KELLEYS ISLAND

An Island Story

By Claudia M. Brown

Project Concept • Development: Sandy Alexander
Design • Claudia Brown

©2007 Kelleys Cove, Inc.

All rights reserved. No part of this book may be reproduced or transmitted in any form or by any means
electronic or mechanical, including photocopying, recording, or by any information storage and retrieval system,
without the written permission from the publisher.

Kelleys Cove, Inc. • P.O. Box 390 • Kelleys Island, Ohio 43438

Dedicated to my parents,
Cecilia Ann (Riedy) Brown and Charles Frederick Brown,
both fourth generation Kelleys Islanders.

Author Claudia Brown with her parents in the early 1950's.

West side of Kelleys Island with Long Point extending to the northeast.

Table of Contents

North bay, Kelleys Island, Ohio

Foreword

Some people have an ownership or genealogical connection or even an emotional relationship with Kelleys Island. I have all three. Both of my parents were born, raised and educated on Kelleys Island and did not live elsewhere until they were adults. While I was not born here, I have had a connection with Kelleys Island my whole life. When I was young, all my relatives lived here, and we came home to Kelleys Island from the Cleveland area for holidays, vacations and week-ends and stayed in the homes of our relatives. I am now the fourth consecutive generation to live on family property (fifth generation on the Island). My parents, as were their parents, were descended from German immigrants who came to Kelleys Island during the nineteenth century. Our families made their living on Kelleys Island for the first three generations as farmers, fishermen, vintners and quarry workers.

Then came the hard times, when the quarry closed, the wine industry faltered before dying, and commercial fishing stopped due to the pollution of Lake Erie. Members of my family had been engaged in all those industries in addition to owning a general store. When it became difficult, then impossible, to find enough work on the Island to sustain family life, the families began to move away. Property values were low in the mid twentieth century, and this became part of the incentive for the rebirth of Kelleys Island into a tourist destination.

New people, many of them retired, began to move to the Island, at least for a few years of their lives. Kelleys Island became a destination, both for the vacationer and for those who wanted to engage in tourist businesses. Many of the large older homes have become bed and breakfasts and been preserved in that way. The Island's once dignified, Western Reserve look of all white houses, with black-trimmed windows and dark green or black shutters has gradually given way to many colored exteriors echoing the "painted lady" look of California's Victorian era homes. What were once cleared fields of grapes, where one could stand almost in the middle of the Island and look down to the lakeshore, have become dense brush and houses and subdivisions.

While the Island's physical appearance and contemporary society have changed greatly from its beginnings, the lure of an Island home endures, and is perhaps stronger today than ever. In today's world of insecurity, the romantic ideas associated with a small community, isolated and hidden from the rest of the world, where everyone knows everyone else by name, has a special pull. Kelleys Island continues to beckon, and people continue to come. Each new group of residents transforms the look and composition of the Island, as it always has.

Floats attached to fishing nets off the south shore with the casino and store dock in the background (early 1900's)

To the Reader

After someone establishes a relationship with Kelleys Island, whether it is as a full time resident, weekender or summer visitor, one begins to refer to Kelleys Island as "The Island", with special emphasis on "Island." Perhaps it is an acknowledgement of the separateness that an island has by virtue of being surrounded by water and therefore cut off from a greater mainland of earth. Perhaps it denotes the recognition of a familiar connection, not only between the speaker and the "island", but also between the speakers themselves. To honor this colloquial use of language, and to give some local flavor to this book, I chose to capitalize "Island" everywhere in the text where the proper name has been shortened and the intent is understood to be Kelleys Island.

In this text, Kelleys Island has been spelled differently depending on the time frame of the reference. After the Kelley family purchased the majority of the Island and renamed it, the spelling was Kelley's Island. This spelling clearly held until around 1900. Sometime later, the apostrophe was dropped, making the current spelling Kelleys Island.

Kelleys Island, longitude N 41° 35' and latitude 82° 42', is the largest United States island in Lake Erie and is situated in the lake's western basin. Pelee Island to the north is larger, but owned by Canada. Kelleys Island is incorporated as a village in Erie County and lies about 12 miles northwest of Sandusky and about five miles north of Lakeside-Marblehead. Kelleys Island had been serviced by ferries coming from Sandusky until Harold Neuman built a dock in Marblehead and started running his ferry boat from there. Today the Island is serviced by Kelleys Island Ferry Boat Lines, Inc. from its dock in Marblehead. The Island is composed of 2,888 acres and is roughly two and a half by four miles in length and breadth. The perimeter of the Island is about eighteen miles long.

The municipality of the Village of Kelleys Island extends two miles from the natural shoreline into the lake, unless curtailed by an existing boundary, such as the boundary between Erie and Ottawa Counties, to the west. The government is a statutory village with eight elected officials: six members of council, a mayor, and a clerk-treasurer. All work part-time in public service to their Kelleys Island community.

The composition of the Island is primarily limestone bedrock from the Devonian Age, about 350 to 400 million years old. At one time the Island had a small river on the south side called the Tiber River. Today the river is channeled through a covered culvert until it flows into Lake Erie.

The climate of Kelleys Island is affected by being surrounded by a large body of water. The spring is cool for a longer period than the nearby mainland, which means that spring flowers may be later to bloom but last longer. The fall is the favorite time of year for many visitors as the lake that has been warming all summer keeps the Island warm. The autumn usually lasts longer than on the mainland. With sugar maples and other deciduous trees dotted amongst the red cedars, the season of color prolongs several weeks longer than other parts of northern Ohio.

Kelleys Island is a stopping place for migratory birds, so many birders come both spring and fall. There is an active Audubon Club that hosts a "Nest with the Birds" program in the spring that attracts visitors from many places, near and far. "Fall Feathers and Foliage" is the autumn program which also includes banding birds.

Pre-History

Glacial Grooves

Geologists estimate that about 18,000 years ago, during the last Ice Age, a huge glacier spread across a large valley, which we now call Lake Erie. Gigantic boulders at the base of the ice scoured into the soft limestone bedrock of the Island, cutting grooves as they traveled. Grooves appear in many places around the Island, especially visible near shorelines where the usual soil covering has been washed away. The most spectacular set of grooves lies at the north end of Division Street, now under the care of the Ohio Historical Society, within the area of Kelleys Island State Park. The Glacial Grooves have been stripped of soil so that it is easier to appreciate their expanse. Originally they were larger, purportedly several miles in length, but the end of them was

Glaciers cut deeply into the island's limestone bedrock and are most visible at the north end of the island.

quarried out. Today they are about 400 feet long, and 35 feet wide, with a groove depth of about 10 feet.

The grooves contain a wonderful fossil record of marine invertebrate animals which once covered the floor of the Devonian Sea about 350 million years ago. Eighteen different kinds of fossils have been identified in the grooves, among them corals, brachipods, gastropods, pelecypods, cephalopods, crinoids and stromato-poroids.

The State maintains a walkway around the uncovered grooves that also crosses over the grooves. In 1949 they were known as the largest and finest example of glacial grooves in the Western Hemisphere. They remain an impressive natural wonder and attract tourists from around the world.

Views of the glacial grooves in the
Kelleys Island State Park

Marine fossils are common on the sedimentary rock which was formed in shallow seas that covered the region more than 350 million years ago.

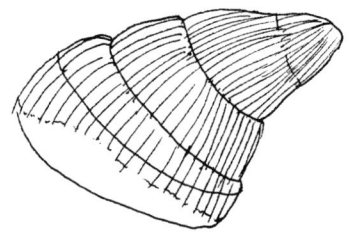

Anthozoa (corals)
"Horn Coral"

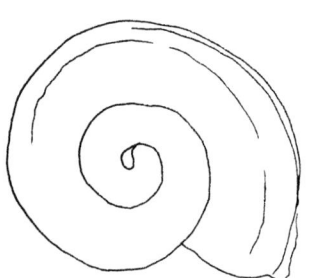

Gastropoda (snail)

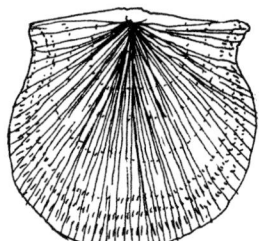

Brochipod – Strophodenta

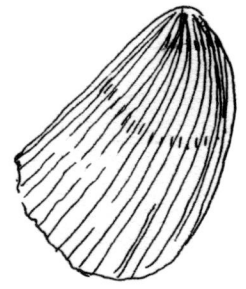

Brochipod – Conchidium

Fossil coral

Trilobite fossil

Glacial grooves are seen in many places along the shoreline. These are at the east end of the island.

Inscription Rock

Inscription Rock as it appears today on the south shore near the intersection of Addison Road and East Lakeshore Drive.

The incised rock was discovered partially buried in 1833 by Charles Olmstead of Connecticut. He had come to the Island to inspect his properties. In 1850 Captain Charles Eastman, of the U.S. Army, came to the Island to make a drawing of the inscriptions for the Bureau of Indian Affairs in Washington, D.C. The top smooth face of the rock contained 122 different pictographs at the time of its discovery. A description of the pictographs was published in 1850, but the first published drawings of the pictographs were in 1852 or 1853. In 1851, copies of the tracings done by Eastman were shown to an Indian named Shingvauk (aka Shingwauk), "Little Pine", to decipher the meaning.

Shingvauk interpreted the pictographs as telling of negotiations, crimes, times of unrest, and incidents of the Erie Indians during their occupation of the Island and the south shore of Lake Erie, although he said that he had no personal knowledge of the exact events. The pictographs also told of the massacre of the Erie Indians by the Iroquois which led to the Erie Nation passing out of existence. The carvings are generally thought to have been done between 1200 and 1600, with the last of them not after 1625, since some of the pictographs have been interpreted to include white men, but without guns. The pictographs on Inscription Rock have been roughly divided into three parts. The largest figure measures eight feet in length. Henry Schoolcraft notes the Inscription Rock as a good example of the "antiquarian period" in his book Indian Antiquities. Exposure to the elements, especially acid rain, has virtually erased the incised drawings. The rock is now under a roof and under the care of the Ohio Historical Society.

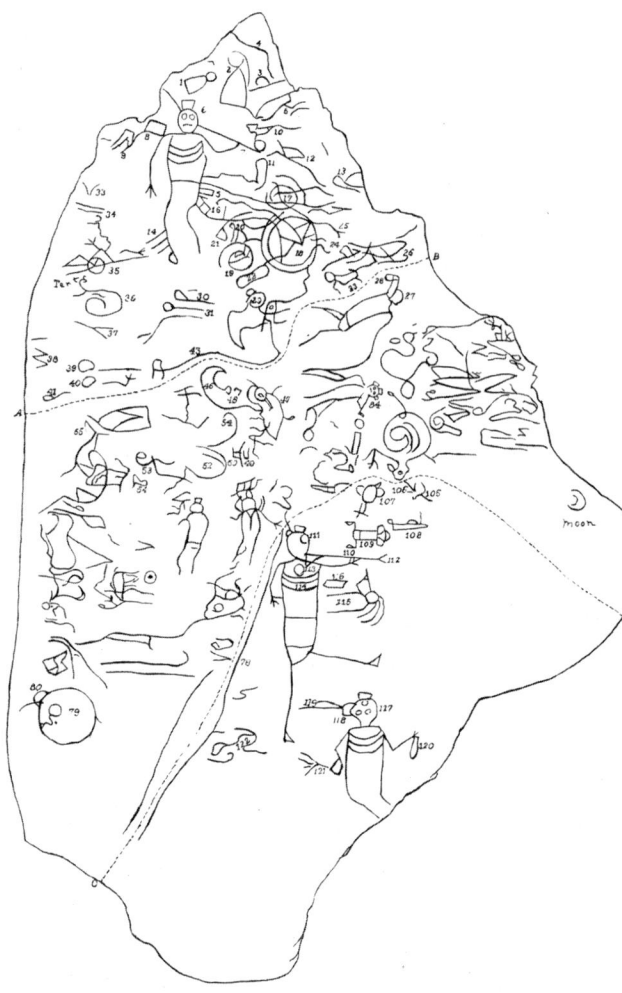

Drawing of the top surface of Inscription Rock as it appeared in 1850.

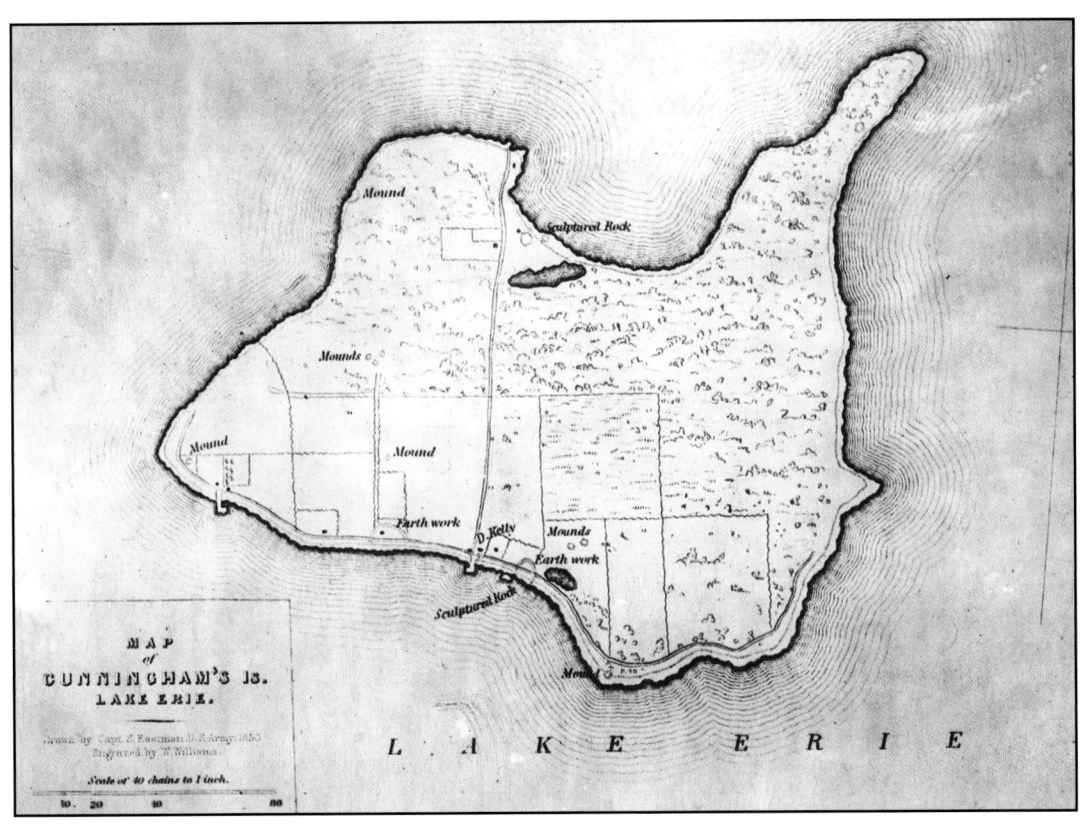

Cunningham's Island (circa 1850)

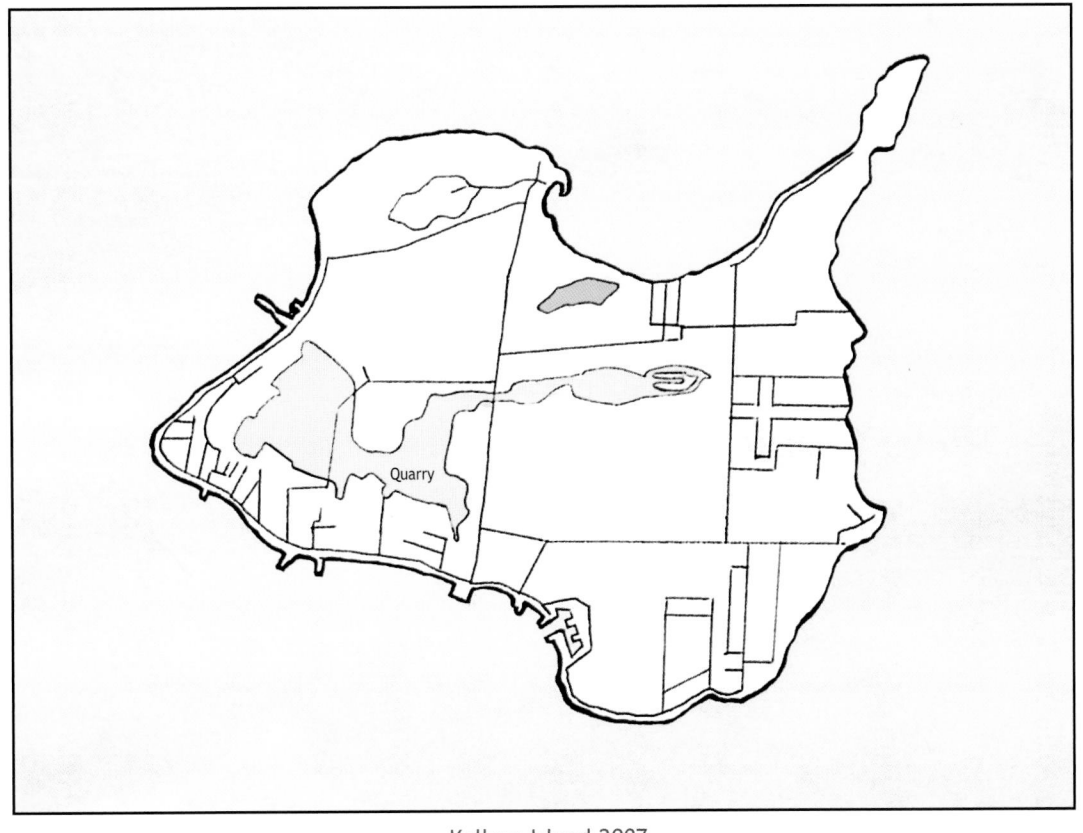

Kelleys Island 2007

Indian Settlements

All authors writing about Kelleys Island history owe gratitude to George C. Huntington who spoke to the Firelands Historical Society on March 11, 1862. At that time he set forth the major points in the Island's history that so many have used since.

In his report Huntington spoke of a long period of occupation of the Island by large numbers of Indians. As evidence of this he cited great numbers of human bones found in ancient burial places, of which he also said there were many. George Huntington built his house about in the center of what had been the largest Indian village. It was the remains of a circular earthwork enclosing about seven acres, according to Erie County histories. Many artifacts were found including numerous flint arrow heads, stone axes, bone fish hooks, pipes, net sinkers and broken bits of pottery. Huntington believed that the Indian earthworks had the same origin as the pictographs on the Island. There was one rock with pictographs on the north side of the Island and one on the south shore (Inscription Rock). Since Huntington first visited the Island on August 7, 1835, and moved to the Island in September of 1838, his research and first hand evidence about native populations is the earliest written record.

The Addison Kelley House, at the corner of Addison Road and East Lakeshore Drive, was also built on the site of an Indian village. There were several mounds in the area which have been excavated. Artifacts such as pottery, grindstones, tomahawks, pipes, arrowheads and flints have been unearthed from the mounds and were also found in nearby fields after plowing.

More recent research by trained anthropologists has added information to the traditional history regarding Native American occupation of the Island. In 1975 an excavation jointly sponsored by Case Western Reserve University and the Cleveland Museum of Natural History was conducted at the Kelley Mansion site. In general, the most meaningful archaeological data uncovered was associated with the Woodland Stage, dating from about 1000 BC to 1500 AD. The Woodland Era generally is characterized as a time of cultural flowering and is distinctive in its practice of burial ceremonialism. Cultural innovations

By 1927, this inscribed rock on the north side was covered by sand.

include the widespread use of pottery and agriculture. Three earthworks, two inscribed rocks and at least fourteen burial mounds have been noted on Kelleys Island.

The Kelley Mansion site was a Late Woodland Village within an earthwork. Evidence of several small semi-permanent structures was found that housed an estimated forty to fifty individuals. Based on the evidence of pottery shards and radiocarbon dating, the site appears to have been occupied from about AD 1300 to AD 1450. There was evidence of mammals and fish having been consumed. Further research into the type of mammals and fish suggested that the occupation of the site was in the spring of the year with the inhabitants moving south to the mainland each summer to plant and tend crops until fall. Winter was spent on the mainland. Native Americans continued to use the Erie islands into the historic period. In 1756, Captain James Smith accompanied Delaware and Canastauga Indians who used the islands as a short cut to Canada. Ottawas and Wyandots are also said to have used the islands. Research suggests that in the 1600's Fr. Louis Hennepin, a French priest, was left on Kelleys Island temporarily by LaSalle. Hennepin eventually traveled further west to the Minnesota area, where his name became prominent in their local history. During the War of 1812, Kelleys Island was too close to the fighting for comfort and neither Indians nor white settlers occupied it. After the War of 1812, both the French and the Indians had been effectively removed from the area and American settlers began to move in, putting an end to any further Indian occupation forever.

1774   On the eve of the American Revolution, the English Parliament made the yet un-named island part of the Province of Quebec, Canada. This designation was in conflict with a land grant made in 1662 by King Charles II of England in which he gave the island to the Colony of Connecticut.

1776   The Declaration of Independence of the United States of America was written.

1778   George Rogers Clark's Campaign of 1778-1779 occupied land north of the Ohio River, capturing forts held by the British.

1781   The British and Tories invaded Connecticut and destroyed nine towns, causing great property losses. In May, 1781, the Connecticut legislature set aside 500,000 acres as compensation to the victims of the destruction. This land was referred to as "Sufferers' Lands" or "Fire Lands". The un-named island, that would eventually be known as Kelleys Island was not included in this land designation as it was still part of Quebec. On October 19, 1781, Cornwallis surrendered his force of 7,000 men to General George Washington at Yorktown.

1783   The Treaty of Paris was signed in which the British formally recognized the independence of the United States.

1785   On January 1, 1785, at Fort McIntosh a treaty was made that gave the islands and other lands west of the Cuyahoga River (at present day Cleveland, Ohio) to the Chippewa, Delaware, Ottawa, and Wyandot Indians. This designated the Cuyahoga River as the western boundary of the United States. The Land Ordinance of 1785 was passed by the Congress of the Confederation and provided that acreage in the "Old Northwest", which included the land destined to become the State of Ohio, should be sold and that the proceeds be used to help pay off the national debt.

1787   Delegates from twelve states convened in Philadelphia to re-write the Articles of Confederation. The Congress passed the Northwest Ordinance that created the Northwest Territory. The ordinance specified how the land in the territory could become states and how the federal government would sell land to private citizens.

1789   George Washington was unanimously elected the first President of the United States.

1790   The last of thirteen states adopted the U.S. Constitution.

1794   The Treaty of Greenville re-confirmed the Cuyahoga River as the western edge of the United States, and gave the land to the west of the river to the Miami Indians and their allies.

1794   With Jay's Treaty the British relinquished all claim to the property that was the south shore of Lake Erie.

        The State of Connecticut ceded its lands to the federal government, retaining the area that came to be known as the Western Reserve. The most western 500,000 acres of this reserve was called the Fire Lands. The remainder of the land was sold to the Connecticut Land Company. Kelleys Island was included in what is known as the Western Reserve but not in the portion known as the Fire Lands.

1796	The Connecticut Land Company sent a party to survey the land for the first time. One of the members of the party, also a shareholder, was Joshua Stow of Middletown, Connecticut. Stow's sister Jemima was the wife of Judge Daniel Kelley, also of Middletown. Daniel Kelley had five sons. Eventually, their Uncle Joshua encouraged them to migrate to the Western Reserve for opportunity. The first to come to the Western Reserve were Datus Kelley and his wife Sara Dean Kelley, her brother Chester Dean and Joshua Reynolds Kelley. They were followed by Alfred, Irad and Thomas Kelley, and then their parents, Daniel and Jemima Kelley. Most settled in Cleveland, Ohio.
1799	On September 24, 1799, part of the Northwest Territory was organized into a state by Governor St.Clair. Ohio was the first state formed from the Northwest Territory.
1800	A map was published of the Ohio country and the island was labeled Cunningham's Island. This indicated that Cunningham had lived on the island prior to 1800 and became acknowledged as the first known white inhabitant.
1801	Thomas Jefferson was inaugurated as President of the United States.
1802	On November 29, 1802, a constitution was adopted and signed by the convention. The State of Ohio was created, becoming a part of the States of the Federal Union, and the island became part of Ohio.
1803	The Louisiana Purchase was made. Jefferson was re-elected President. Ohio became the seventeenth state of the United States of America.
1804	Lewis and Clark began their exploration of the west.
1805	On July 4, 1805, the Indians gave up claim to the lands to the west of the Cuyahoga River in the Treaty of Fort Industry.

Food, supplies and livestock arrived over thick ice in the winter.

1807   The first survey was done, and it is assumed that the islands were included. The island was designated as "Island Number Six", also known as "Cunningham's Island." The land was attached to Township No. 5 to make the township of equal average value as other townships for the investors of the Connecticut Land Company. The majority of Township No. 5 was on the mainland and was eventually split into several jurisdictions.

1809   Huron County, Ohio, was formed, which originally covered the area known as the "Fire Lands." In his book, A History of Kelley's Island, Ohio, Norman E. Hills quoted historian Howe that the name Huron was the French name for the Wyandot Indians who occupied most of the area.

1810   Cunningham, and Frenchmen Bebo and Pochile were cutting wood on Cunningham's Island. Bebo made a small clearing near the West Bay and built a cabin facing west. Pochile cleared a site on the south shore, a little west of the largest of the ancient Indian villages. The George C. Huntington house was eventually located about in the center of this Indian village.

1812   Cunningham, Bebo, and Pochile were attacked by Indians on the island, and they escaped to the mainland. This was about the time of the Indian raid on the south shore of Lake Erie after the surrender of Detroit. Cunningham died of his wounds, but the island would be known as Cunningham's Island for another twenty years. Between this year and 1818, no settlers were mentioned as inhabitants on the island.

    Irad Kelley bought a farm near Green Springs, Ohio. When the Indians raided near his land, he went to Cleveland, Ohio.

Narrow-gauge Shay engines traveled the length of the West Bay stone loading dock.

1812	In June of 1812, war was declared between the United States and England. Commanders on both sides of the conflict anticipated a naval battle for control of Lake Erie. U.S. naval forces led by Commodore Oliver Hazard Perry assembled on the south shore of Kelleys Island. Perry's fleet received supplies and recruits from mainland Ohio. General William Henry Harrison visited Commodore Perry there to discuss strategy for the approaching battle. When the fleet left the area, a small encampment of men was left on the west side of the island at Bebo's clearing near present day West Bay. They had a small sailboat, and their duty was to report any movements of the British fleet on the lake to Gen. Harrison. Hills wrote that possibly these men built the small dock that was later shown on a map of the island included among General Perkin's papers. Hills continued that the site of this encampment was unearthed before 1925 as workmen were removing top soil in preparation for quarrying stone. Old tent stakes were found among the bones of several human skeletons and also some old army uniform buttons and a few musket barrels with the date of 1812.
1813	September 11, 1813, Commodore Perry engaged the British fleet near South Bass Island, just west of Kelleys Island. Perry's battle flag proclaimed "Don't Give Up the Ship." Perry lost his own flagship but prevailed and captured the entire British fleet of six ships. Perry's victory secured the Great Lakes for U.S. forces which allowed General Harrison's troops to safely cross Lake Erie to recapture Detroit. South Bass Island, eight miles to the west of Kelleys Island, today hosts the tall white column that is Perry's Victory and International Peace Memorial, which can be clearly seen from the west shore of Kelleys Island.
1815	The War of 1812 ended.
1815-1817	Cunningham's Island was designated as part of Danbury Township, Huron County, Ohio.
1817	When a controversy arose between the Connecticut Land Company and the Fire Lands people, a number of islands in Lake Erie reverted to the Connecticut Land Company, among them Island Number Six, also known as Cunningham's Island. It was decided that the shore line of Lake Erie would be the northern limit of the Fire Lands. Island Number Six, or Cunningham's Island, was divided into thirteen lots of unequal size and distributed as compensation amongst the shareholders of the Connecticut Land Company who had been shorted on their original land portion. James Monroe was inaugurated as President of the United States.
1818	Habitation returned to the island. Cunningham's Island became a regular refueling stop for the first steamboat on Lake Erie, the *Walk-in-the-Water.* There was no dock on the island and the cut red cedar wood used for fuel had to be ferried out to the steamboat using smaller boats. A man named Killiam and his family lived on the island, along with at least two other men, Barnum and Grummetts. All engaged in supplying firewood to the steamboat. Freight and passengers moved between Sandusky City, on the mainland, and the islands by small sailboat. Killiam cleared several acres of land on the south shore to the east of where Division Street divides the island today. Killiam divided his lot into six parts and built his house on the area previously cleared by Pochile, about one half mile west of his own clearing.
	Captain Coit used a small sail boat to transport people and freight between the islands and the mainland.
1820	The *Walk-in-the-Water* was wrecked and Killiam and Coit moved away from the island as their commerce ended with the ship wreck. James Monroe was re-elected President of the United States.

Kelleys Island's rocky shoreline on the southwest, with Catawba and Mouse Island on the horizon.

1820-1826   Barnum and Grummets, who were previously employed by Killiam, were cutting wood to sell. Barnum built a cabin on the east point of the island, near the east end of present day Woodford Road. The area had been known as Barnum's Point, then Woodford's Point after Woodford bought the property, and then Hamilton's Point when the Hamilton family owned it. In 1826 Barnum killed Grummets while they were alone on the island.

1827   Elisha Ellis and his wife and Sam Beardsley and his wife were the only inhabitants of the island. Mrs. Beardsley died in February, 1827, and was buried on the shore of the island. It is from this period forward that continuous habitation began on the island.

1828   General Andrew Jackson defeated John Quincy Adams to become President.

Henry Ellithorpe came to the island to raise livestock. In the same year, two nieces of Mrs. Ellis were visiting her and got sick. One of the nieces, Miss Kellogg, died on the island and was buried next to Mrs. Beardsley. The other niece, Miss Brooks, was taken to Sandusky where she also died. Mr. and Mrs. Ellis, Mr. Ellithorpe and Frank Saunders, employed by Ellis, were the only inhabitants of the island. In 1829 Ira B. Henderson and his family lived temporarily on the island.

1829   In the winter of 1829-1830 the only inhabitants were Mr. and Mrs. Ellis, Henry Ellithorpe and E.T. Smith, known as "Tinker" Smith.

1830   Nicholas Haskins, his wife and eight or nine children lived near the pond on the south shore. This was later known as Kelley Pond and is the site of the Seaway Marina today. The location had previously been known as the "Old Burying Ground" because of the Indian mounds in the immediate area. Luther Ludd, his wife and four children built a house on the larger Indian Village site. In December, 1830, Ellithorpe married Elizabeth Neale in Sandusky and brought his bride to the island by sleigh over the ice. He also brought six head of cattle. Ellithorpe built his cabin on the southeast shore of Great Lot 10.

1832   October 6, 1832 the first white child, Cyrus Ellithorpe, was born on the island. During the 1830's McGuffey's First Eclectic Reader was published.

1833   Benjamin A. Napier came to the island with his family and five or six men. He claimed to own the island. Previously, Napier is said to have been ejected from South Bass Island by its inhabitants. Napier moved into the house formerly occupied by Ellis and Ellis moved into a house shared with someone else. Napier appropriated livestock owned by Ellis and others and was said to have established his rights by force.

Honorable John W. Allen of Cleveland, Ohio, who represented General Perkins, the agent of the Connecticut Land Company, had been in Norwalk, Ohio trying to sell a portion of Cunningham's Island. After his return to Cleveland, he mentioned the island to Irad Kelley.

On July 12, 1833 Irad and Datus Kelley visited Cunningham's Island. Hills wrote that "it is probable that they interviewed Ellis, Clemens, and others on the island regarding their tenancy..." The inhabitants on the island made no claims of ownership.

On August 20, 1833 Datus and Irad Kelley, brothers from Cleveland, Ohio began to invest in almost 1,500 of the 2,888 acres known as Cunningham's Island. The vast deposits of high quality limestone and abundant cedar forests were purchased for $1.50 an acre. There appears to have been some changes to the first contract for the island property and Charles A. Olmsted of Connecticut was sent to make new arrangements with the Kelley brothers. At the same time, Mr. Olmsted visited the

The Bass Islands are easily seen from the west side of Kelleys Island

island and discovered "Inscription Rock" on the south shore. After completing the original purchase of land on the island, Irad Kelley asked his brother Datus to send stone from the island to Cleveland that would be suitable for fireplace mantels, fireplaces, jambs and stones for a cemetery monument for his father. This stone was used for the family house that he was completing in Cleveland. Luther Dodge and his family accompanied Datus Kelley from Rockport to Kelleys Island. The Dodge family then operated the first Kelley company boarding house.

Irad Kelley   Datus Kelley

Oberlin College in Ohio admitted women for the first time as students.

Late in the fall, during his absence, Datus Kelley put Luther Dodge temporarily in charge of cutting wood to be used for steamboat fuel and building docks.

1834   Julius Kelley, second son of Datus Kelley, was put in charge of affairs at the island in his father's absence. Datus and Irad Kelley had a 106 ton schooner built in Rocky River, Ohio named *Ben Franklin*. She was launched in June and sold in Buffalo the following spring (1835). The

DIVISION ST. KELLEY'S ISLAND OHIO. 1912

Chadwick family, also from Rockport, succeeded the Dodge family in running the company boarding house. By fall of 1834, Mrs. Knowlton was the landlady of the boarding house. Stone quarried and shipped from Kelleys Island was valued at $800, and the red cedar posts and pork totaled $400. Stone monuments were sold for the Ohio Indiana State line. The stone was shipped from a dock on the north side of the island, a short distance west of the opening for the North Bay. Mr. John Clemens had been quarrying stone in 1833 on the island and probably built the dock. Clemens moved to Marblehead where he continued in the stone business.

1835   In January, Addison Kelley, son of Datus Kelley, was named as his father's agent in charge of the island property for the family firm. In a letter, Addison Kelley mentioned four houses on Kelleys Island: those of Henry Ellithorpe, Elisha Ellis, Benjamin Napier, and the two room log cabin that was the company boarding house, run by Mrs. Knowlton. E.T. Smith was one of the boarders. In November, 1835, a sheriff's deputy moved the Napier family off the island. Napier went to the Norwalk court and his family went to North Bass Island. Addison Kelley built a large log house on the west side of Division Street, about 1500 feet from the south lake shore. The property was later sold to George Kelley, who enlarged it, and used part of it as a store. The house still stands in its original location and is currently Janice's Antiques.

Janice's Antiques, the oldest house on Kelleys Island.

1836   By 1836, the Kelley brothers had purchased most of the island. Datus Kelley employed workers to cut wood for steamboats and to build a dock on the south side of the island, at the end of present day Division Street. At this time both of the Kelley brothers, Datus and Irad, resided off the island. Irad lived in a mansion on Euclid Avenue in Cleveland, Ohio, and Datus had a farm west of Rocky River, Ohio. It was reported that there were twelve families on the island in addition to unmarried men; not all the names were mentioned. In an article in *The Islander* about Jake Hay, some names were given of islanders at the time of Jake Hay's arrival in 1836. They were Mrs. Knowlton, families of Henry Harris, Patrick Martin, Barney McGettigan, Isaac Rice; and single men—Addison Kelley, Jake Hay, Ephrain T. Smith. Datus Kelley moved to the island with his family in either 1836 (Hermon Kelley's family history) or 1837 (Addison Kelley's autobiography in *The Islander*). The first sale of real estate was made by Datus and Irad Kelley to Addison Kelley.

1836   Texans declared independence from Mexico and fought at the Alamo. Martin Van Buren was elected the eighth President of the United States.

1837   Kelleys Island became part of Erie County, transferred from Danbury Township, Huron County. Addison Kelley began a house on the lake bank, east side of Division Street, overlooking the dock. The men employed in the house's construction were J.E. Woodford, as boss carpenter, and Joseph Willet, stone mason. This house was the first framed house, but the second framed building, after a school house. The house was sold and eventually destroyed by fire.

1838   George C. Huntington moved to the island. There were already twelve families on the island: Datus Kelley, Addison Kelley, P. Martin, Henry Harris, Joseph Willett, Mrs. Knowlton, Barney

The Island House was built in the 1860's to accommodate the burgeoning tourist trade. A community park now occupies the location.

McGettigan, George Firkins, H. Bickford, John Titus, J. Jubenville and Sumner Knapp. Jacob Hay boarded with Mrs. Knowlton.

1839   Sailboat *Boat "No. 1"* was built and served as the main transport until the steamer *Islander* was built in 1846.

1840   William Henry Harrison was elected President of the United States.

1842   On May 17, 1842, Datus and Irad Kelley finally received deeds for the Joseph Perkins property on the island.

1840-1845   From March 6, 1840 to December 31, 1845, the island was part of Ottawa County and was known as Kelley's Island Township. Sixty-eight people lived on the island, but only 15 votes were polled in the first election. Island industry was primarily quarrying, wood cutting, commercial fishing, and farming. The biggest cash crop was the exportation of wheat. The Kelley family began planting grape vines. Most of the island's commerce passed through the Sandusky Bay area in Erie County, and the residents of the island petitioned to become part of Erie County.

1845   Ireland had a potato famine and many people immigrated to the United States.

1846   On January 1, 1846 the Township of Kelley's Island was transferred back to Erie County, with Sandusky City as the county seat for the island. The *Islander* steamboat, built on the south shore of the island from native timber, began service and was used to transport wheat from the island. War began between Mexico and the U.S. on April 25th, 1846 and ended February 2, 1848.

1848   Wars in Germany caused an exodus of Germans to the U.S. and gold was discovered in California.

1850   The Underground Railroad stepped up activity transporting Negro slaves through Ohio, from Sandusky to Canada and freedom.

1853	The *Island Queen* was built on the island and towed to Sandusky to have an engine installed. This boat allowed for scheduled transportation of passengers, products, and mail three times a week. Between 1849 and 1863, the island's population grew from 180 to 600 residents.
1857	James Buchanan became President. On March 6, 1857, the Dred Scott decision was made by the Supreme Court.
1859	John Brown was caught in a raid at Harper's Ferry, Virginia.
1860	Abraham Lincoln was elected President, and southern states began to secede from the Union.
1861	The Civil War began. Men from Kelleys Island became soldiers.
1862	Grape rot destroyed half of the grape crop on Kelleys Island.
1865	The Civil War ended, and President Lincoln was assassinated.
1876	Rutherford B. Hayes from Ohio was elected to the Presidency of the United States.
1881	James A. Garfield of Ohio became President.
1884	Grover Cleveland of Ohio was elected President of the United States.
1887	On July 27, 1887, the Township of Kelley's Island was incorporated into the Village of Kelley's Island, in Erie County. The municipality included all of the island's land mass and extended two miles into the lake. The northern extension of the Village of Kelleys Island was the international boundary line between the United States and Canada. In the register of incorporation the apostrophe in Kelley's Island was but a dot on the page, perhaps a harbinger of its eventual loss sometime after 1900.

Looking north from Koster's Dock.

Vineyard, Kellys Island, O.

Kelleys Island was once covered in vineyards.

The Kelley Family

The Kelley brothers descended from Scotch Presbyterians, and were deeply concerned about the religious and educational welfare of their community. They were community planners and built schools, a town center with a large hall (Kelley Hall known as the town hall today), and docks, housing for employees, and a hotel. The Kelleys operated businesses from their Island properties, engaging in the sale of red cedar timber, a native tree on the Island, the quarrying of limestone, and the manufacture of wine. Red cedar still grows all over the Island, and the quarry has expanded and gone in and out of business over the years, but is still functioning. Unfortunately the grape growing and wine industries are no longer commercially viable.

In describing the history of Kelleys Island, Norman Kelley is purported to have said that "Kelley's Island was originally inhabited by rattlesnakes, that the hogs came and ate the rattlesnakes, then the Irish came and ate the hogs, then the Germans came and drove out the Irish." And that is a colorful summary of the history of Kelleys Island up to about 1900.

Wine Industry

The Kelley family planted Isabella and Concord vines as early as 1841, but it was Charles Carpenter, married to Caroline Kelley, who first realized the commercial value of viticulture. Carpenter purchased 123 acres on the southwest corner of the Island from Horace Kelley in 1846 and planted Catawba grapes. The vines were slow to mature but produced an excellent quality grape. The Catawba vines were so productive in the north coast area, that a nearby mainland peninsula bears their name—Catawba Island. The cultivation of grapes and production of wine was so successful that it caused a dramatic increase in residents and a boom in housing construction. Carpenter had a successful presentation of his wine at the 1853 Ohio State Fair and was so encouraged that he built the first winery north of Cincinnati, Ohio. Using stone from his former quarry, Carpenter built a huge wine cellar. Kelleys Island wines won state, national, and international competitions. The soil was very good along the southern and eastern shores of the Island and in the Sweet Valley region, and these became the major grape production areas. The climate of the Island was suit-

19

ed to grape production, even though it is farther north than is usually viable. The lake kept the Island warm late into the fall and thus made a sufficiently long growing season for grapes to mature, and lake breezes helped counter vine rot and mildew.

Starting in the 1850's, the Island attracted many immigrants from the grape growing areas of Germany. The Germans came because of political upheavals and failures of the European grape crops. In 1872, about 25 independent, small farmers were producing grapes for wine making. Most of the wineries remained small, family operations.

In 1880 John Schaedler bought land, and by 1887 he had built a winery with a cellar capacity of 15,000 gallons. Louis Rhein, a wine maker from the Alsace area of France became an equal partner with Schaedler in 1892 and their business became one of the largest producers on the Island with a cellar capacity of 80,000 gallons. One third of the grapes needed for production were harvested from their 28 acre company vineyard. While the winery was closed during Prohibition, both Schaedler and Rhein died.

Between 1865 and Prohibition in 1919, the wine regions of Erie and Ottawa counties were consistently ranked first or second in wine production in the state of Ohio. The same weather and soil conditions that favor grapes are also good for fruit trees. Eventually some of the vineyards became fruit orchards, as the vines aged and the wine market changed. Fruit, however, never became a viable cash crop.

By 1865, there was more competition in the wine industry, and a cooperative was established named the Kelley's Island Wine Company. Smaller vineyards were encouraged to sell their grapes to the newly formed company. The larger company could more efficiently market the wines than the individual winery owner could, and thus increase profits for everyone. The cooperative rented cellar space from Charles Carpenter. By 1871, with new cellar construction, the total storage capacity was 400,000 gallons. Champagne production was begun, and at the Philadelphia Centennial Exposition of 1876, the Kelley's Island Wine Company received the Diploma of Highest Merit and the Grand Medal of Honor for its champagne. Kelley's Island Wine Company products were marketed internationally. Champagnes such as Island Queen and La Rein de L'Isle, as well as dry and sweet Catawbas, Reislings, ports, and clarets were shipped throughout the United States, Canada, Great Britain and Germany.

The turn of the century in 1900 brought increased competition from production in neighboring states and California. This came at a time when the vineyards were aging, the soil fertility had decreased, and the original vintners were retiring and passing away. Mainland Sandusky had rail service which was faster and more economical than boat transport from the Island, and so some wine production moved there. In 1913, A. F. Elfers recorded that there were six large wineries and four brandy distilleries on Kelleys Island. In 1910, over 11,000 gallons of brandy was distilled. The final end to wineries on Kelleys Island came with the enactment of Prohibition in 1919. Of the five wineries still in operation, only the Kelley's Island Wine Company was able to change from the production of wine to grape juice, but a fire in 1933 left the buildings in ruins. The company had been able to withstand earlier fires

AUGUSTUS SHAEDLER'S RESIDENCE.
KELLY'S ISLAND.
1874

The Schaedler residence and winery were located on the southeast shore. Both buildings are still standing. The house is easily identified by the family name in the peak. Today the winery building forms the entrance to Gorchester's Southaven subdivision.

The Monarch Winery Co., operated by Roland Brown into the 1950's, was the last winery to close. It used the same building that had previously been the Sweet Valley Wine Co., started by a relative, Otto Brown.

in 1876 and 1915, but the 1933 fire and lack of market made the venture no longer viable.

Before the Civil War the Jacob Rush Winery had a cellar near north bay. In 1872 Rush built a new cellar on Division Street in the area known as Sweet Valley.

The new cellar was built of native limestone, had two stories, and a capacity of 70,000 gallons. A distillery was located at the back of the winery. The Rush Winery was sold to Otto Brown in 1879, who operated it as the Otto Brown Winery. Brown enlarged the existing building and increased the capacity to 140,000 gallons, making it the second largest wine cellar on the Island. Four wine presses were in utilization. In 1887 Brown merged his business with other Islanders, R.R. Moysey, Henry Trieschman, Frederick Kastning and Adam Miller to form a joint stock company, known as the Sweet

Valley Wine Company. The company employed six men. After the Civil War and until about 1920, the annual wine production averaged about a half million gallons. Most of the 150 acres of winery vineyards were located near the winery in Sweet Valley. This was an era of wine as an art.

Otto Brown's grandson Charles spoke of following his grandfather around the vineyards as a child, watching him taste different herbs growing at the foot of grape rows, some used with the wine and some used to help determine the readiness and quality of the grapes. Otto Brown managed the company until about 1900. It was then reformed as the Monarch Wine Company, the only winery to re-open after Prohibition, and operated until about 1950. The ruins of the winery building are still visible from Division Street on private property.

Leon Heinl's watercolor of the Kelley's Island Winery Co. as it appeared before being destroyed by fire.

There are many remnants of old wineries left standing. These are ruins of Monarch Wine Co., one of the many independent wine companies that once flourished on Kelleys Island. They are easily seen from Division St.

The house directly to the north of the winery ruins was built for Otto Brown in 1892 as his family home. It remained in the Brown family until 1984. For a few years, subsequent owners, the Johnsons, operated the Queen Anne style house as a bed and breakfast and named it the Sweet Valley Inn. They eventually sold the house and it returned to private use.

The exterior of the Otto Brown house was changed from all white to yellow and white in the second half of the twentieth century. It is one of the few historic homes that did not suffer major renovations.

Tourism

In the nineteenth century, Kelleys Island wineries were a popular destination for many summer excursion boats. In addition to the wineries, hotels, guest houses, and private homes often produced their own wine during the era from the late 1860's to the early twentieth century. Some wineries also served food in their wine tasting areas. One of these was the West Bay Inn, originally part of the Schaedler and Rhein Winery. The winery building was purchased in 1935, renovated, and re-named Kamp Kellile. It operated as a bar and restaurant, with a dance band on Saturday nights in the summer. The north side addition to the building dates from the 1900's. The private marina in front of West Bay Inn was built for the original winery and its guests.

In recent times, the Zettler family moved to the Island and copyrighted the name Kelley's Island Wine Company for their label. They started a winery in 1981 on land that was once part of the nineteenth century Beatty vineyards and the Nicholas Smith winery. From their Vinifera and French Hybrid grapes, Zettler's Kelley's Island Wine Company has produced a variety of wines on their 12 acres situated towards the middle of the Island on Woodford Road. Kirt Zettler continues to make wine on the premises. The business has expanded to include a wine tasting room, a bar and restaurant, and open air dining in a family atmosphere.

In the mid 1800's, steamship lines operating between Detroit and Buffalo sometimes dropped passengers at Kelleys Island instead of going into Sandusky. The passengers would then have to book passage on *The Islander* to complete their trip. Meanwhile, they needed food and accommodations. The Datus Kelley house on the northeast corner of Division and Water Streets (now East Lakeshore Drive) was the only house large enough for these unexpected visitors. To meet this demand, a three story addition was added to the house. Addison Kelley and his wife officially opened a 107 room hotel, The Island House, in the spring of 1853. By the 1860's steamboats traveled regularly between Detroit and Sandusky and would routinely stop at Kelleys Island to discharge and pick up passengers and freight. During the summer there was also weekly service between Cleveland and Kelleys Island. Spring and fall were popular for hunting and fishing, and midsummer for family vacations. In 1866 Addison Kelley moved to his new stone mansion uphill from Inscription Rock, at the corner of Addison and Water Streets. In 1866, after the death of Datus Kelley, the Island House was first sold to a group of investors, and later to Jacob Rush. Running water was put into the hotel when Rush owned it, along with other improvements. After the summer season in 1877, the Island House was destroyed by fire. Jacob Rush was ruined financially by the fire and he moved off the Island, to Kansas. The hotel was re-built, only to burn to the ground again. The lot remained vacant until purchased by the Kel-Isle Civic Club and given to the Village. The land was dedicated as a village park during the Memorial Day festivities of 1924.

The Schardt House and the Himmelein House were two other hotels on Water Street (now East Lakeshore Drive); both established in the 1870's. The Himmelein House was built by Johann and Johanna Himmelein and was expanded several times. It included a bowling alley in a separate building to the east of the hotel, and a saloon.

Beginning in the 1880's, the Howard Wall Model Comedy Company used the Himmelein hotel in the summer to study their seasonal repertoire. The actors practiced at Kelleys Hall (the town hall), around the corner on Division Street and then they gave performances—what we would call "summer stock" today. Through that connection, the Himmelein's son John became an advance theatrical agent. At the end of August each year, John Himmelein and his wife would leave the Island to follow the theatre circuit. The Himmelein House closed in 1916, but is still used as a summer home by family descendants.

Since the nineteenth century, Kelleys Island has maintained its reputation as a quiet restful summer place to which visitors want to return year after year. Today the local attractions revolve around nature and history. Indians used the Island as a crossing place between Canadian and United States shores, carving their stories into Inscription Rock. The ice-age glacial grooves enchanted the nineteenth century visitor as well as those of today. The warm summer breezes and gently lapping water along the shoreline have soothed many a weary traveler or city dweller, and today calm the spirit of the harried businessman. In the nineteenth century, visitors stayed at hotels and tourist homes, usually taking their meals at the same place, and walked, boated, toured in horse drawn buggies, and visited the wine cellars to sample the local vintages. Today there is a choice of bed and breakfasts, motels, cabins, condo rentals and camping. The Ohio State Park ensures that some green space will always be visible, and includes a variety of walking paths through old quarry, wooded, and water areas. For tourists who are used to walking, the Island is small enough to walk anywhere and safe enough to do so. The downtown is concentrated at the southern foot of Division Street, at the lake's edge, with a few additional restaurants around the west side. The Island hosts a lively bar/restaurant scene, but is primarily still a quiet place where you can curl up with a book on a porch, nap on Sand Beach, or meditate on the endless rhythm of waves rolling into shore.

Bed and breakfast establishments really developed in the 1970's. Before that, visitors could rent a room, with meals, in a few homes on the Island, and probably had dinner with the family. The bed and breakfast of today may be in a luxurious modern house with spas, or a nineteenth century Victorian home complete with period furnishings. Most are on the lakeshore or in historic neighborhoods. They cater to guests, some offering gardens or services such as spa massages. Some of the historic homes that are now bed and breakfasts are Carriage House Bed and Breakfast (Norman Kelley, 1857), The Inn on Kelleys Island (Erastus Huntington, 1876), Cricket Lodge (John Himmelein, 1906), Zettler's Lakefront rentals (William Burger, 1897), and Jorski's Cameron House (1860, with 1887 Queen Anne addition). Morning Glory Farm off McGettigan Road is a historic house that was moved from Ward Road by the Robert Paine family to its current lakeside location. The house was originally the residence of the Rev. Robert McCune (1867). The Rev. McCune also used his home for Congregational church services and meetings, until the new Congregational church was built on Division Street in 1877.

Authors have come to Kelleys to write, and artists to paint. Dr. Walter Havighurst, chair of the Department of Literature of Miami University, Oxford, Ohio, wrote a number of books about Lake Erie and the Great Lakes, and he wrote a novel, Signature of Time, while summering on the Island.

At first, vacationers would come and stay for a week at one of the Island's small private hotels or tourist homes. The first summer people to have permanent quarters were affluent Cleveland attorneys, and they had homes that were in family compounds on large acreage, notably the Minshall family on the northwest corner of the Island, and the Jones family that owned all of Long Point to the northeast. Mabel Rice Minshall visited Kelleys Island as a girl, and when she married William E. Minshall, they spent part of their honeymoon on the Island. When the Kelleys Island Lime & Transport Co. went out of business, the Minshall and Jones families purchased property. Several generations of Minshalls and Jones summered on the Island, with only the Minshall family holding property to this day and becoming residents. William E. Minshall III was Mayor of Kelleys Island, 1996-1999. His brother Werner Minshall has served on the Village Planning Commission for several terms. All types of tourism have increased, but especially noticeable is the increase in the number of daily visitors, those that arrive in the morning and leave in the afternoon.

Tourists arriving at Seaway Marina

Goodtime I at the Casino dock

Late afternoon at Portside Marina

Visiting boats anchored at a south side private dock

Vacation Homes

The former inhabitants of Kelleys Island were local fishermen, small businessmen, quarry workers and farmers. Over time "traditional" Kelleys Island began to be sought by urbanites as a break from their daily routine and as a place to restore one's spirit. The new residents had both disposable income and many had no real family connections to the Island. At present, the summer residents compose more than 75% of the Island's population.

After remaining basically unchanged for many years, the development of property to cater to summer residency seemed to come suddenly. The desire to have your own vacation cabin ignited an idea that is still vital today, owning a "piece of the rock." The sub-division of land into vacation home sites began. At first everyone wanted to be on the lake shore, then gradually the more interior land also became attractive. In fact, some investors saw the business potential of tourism early in the twentieth century. From the 1920's onwards, the Island has been promoted as a destination for summer recreational activities. After Lester Carpenter died, Mr. A. D. Wiese purchased the Carpenter property at the southwestern tip of the Island. In 1919 he marked out lot lines for his proposed subdivision and in 1922 he re-subdivided the property as Carpenter Grove Allotment No. 2, which includes Mildred, Erie and Beach Roads. All those roads start at Water Street (now known as West Lakeshore Drive). Not many lots sold and all that remains today of his development are brick boundary markers along West Lakeshore Drive. Another early west side subdivision, plat dated March 1924, was the Richards Subdivision, that includes Forest, Pauline, Etta, Richards and Parkwood Streets. A few small summer cottages were constructed along the Island shoreline during the 1930's and 1940's, mostly on the south side. Around 1944, Howard Navorska purchased the Carpenter House and surrounding property which he subdivided around 1954 to make home, cottage, and trailer sites, and streets, naming it Sunset Point, by which it is still known today. This remains the only privately owned trailer park on the Island.

In 1949, development started on the north side of the Island, with the Kaempfe Subdivision, in the north bay area. In 1950, the Village Clerk estimated the number of tourists at 1,000 for that year. Today's estimates reach 200,000 visitors annually.

In 1957, Hunter and Cruse subdivided property along a farmer's lane, once known as Beatty Lane and then Schlesselman's Lane, and renamed the road Harbor Lane. Cruse came to the Island to work on the marina and decided to invest with family members in making a subdivision. Lake Court, off Harbor Lane, was platted in 1963. The general area became a major area of development along the southeast corner of the Island, the area now called Sweetbriar after the subdivision of that name. The Sweetbriar plat was first done around 1957-58. Prior to subdivision developments, roads were named after the original families living on them. With subdividing, some of the roads changed their names. Some roads however, kept their historic names, like Monagan (Monaghan family), McGettigan, Woodford, Ward and Bookerman (originally Bokerman).

With the economic affluence of the 1950's there was a major shift from the tourism of cottage rental to cottage ownership, and many families still connected to the Island trace their beginnings back to that era when their cottage was purchased and they began the weekly ritual of leaving their main home and coming to the Island on week-ends. A new open design in ferry boats serving the Island also made it easier for families to bring their own cars, being able to easily drive them on and off the boat. Operating from Marblehead, instead of Sandusky, also allowed people to have a shorter lake journey (about 20 to 25 minutes instead of over an hour) to reach the south shore of the Island. This shorter distance is especially welcome if the lake is rough. During the 1950's some of the permanent (year-round) residents opened their homes to tourists, by renting rooms to them, usually with full meals included, as there was

4-H camp on Ward Road

not yet much commercial development in the way of restaurants.

Areas have continued to be developed for second homes through the years, with the trend continuing strong into the twenty-first century. In the 1990's the affluence in the U.S. economy translated to further development on Kelleys Island. One of the major differences between the 1950's summer home and that of today is that the new second homes are getting bigger and bigger every year, and they are generally built as year-round structures even if they are planned only for summer use.

Camps

Many people had their first experience on Kelleys Island as children at one of the summer camps situated here. The Four H Club of Erie County acquired a 65 acre tract of land with a house on the north side of the Island in 1945 through the vision of a group of Erie County farmers. The property runs from Ward Road on the south side to the lake on its north. Erie County 4-H has been responsible for the camp since 1952. Bloomingville Grange of Erie County donated a huge bell to the 4-H Camp to be used to signal session changes and meal times. At first tents were used for the campers, but around the mid-1950's cabins were built. The early 1960's saw a recreation hall added, and a nature education center was added in the early 1990's. The sandy beach along the north shore of the property has been a major attraction to the campers which allows the camp to feature water activities such as fishing and snorkeling. The 4-H Camp hosts members of 4-H, Girl Scouts, band camps, and church groups during the summer months, and is open to all ages, although the majority of the campers are from nine to thirteen years old. The 4-H Club continues to develop the property and hosts about 2,500 children and adults every summer, June through August, from all over the State of Ohio.

Father Vaclav Chaloupka came to Kelleys Island to celebrate mass for the Slovaks that lived on the Island and worked in the quarries. He became familiar with the Island and in 1923 he purchased the property that had been the Samuel and Robert Hamilton house (c. 1860). The central stone part of the building was the homestead of Samuel and Eliza Hamilton, both from Tyrone, Ireland. They came to the Island in 1839, and were some of the first to purchase land from the Kelleys. In 1851, Samuel Hamilton's parents purchased land adjacent to his, to the north, at the base of Long Point. After their parents' death, Robert and his widowed sister Ann Hamilton Brown lived in the house. Robert was a successful grape farmer. Through tragedies, two children were orphaned in the Selfe family and the Hamilton brother and sister took them into their home. In later life, James Selfe, one of the orphans and his wife Lydia lived in the house.

Father Chaloupka made the six acre parcel into a children's camp. When Father Chaloupka was assigned to Cleveland's Nativity of The Blessed Virgin Mary Parish, he brought the summer camp with him. During its years of operation, the "Villa", as it was known, gave hundreds of children a respite from hot city streets for a week in the summer. Children could work at the camp and then have a partial scholarship. Every night there was a big bonfire and entertainment by the campers. Eventually it became hard for Father Chaloupka to maintain the camp and he sold the property to the Ohio Regular Baptist Home and Camp, Inc. in 1952 and it was re-named Camp Patmos.

Camp Patmos on Monagan Road

Almost immediately improvements were begun: a chapel (1959), a pool (1968), miniature lighthouse (1971), new cabins for girls and boys (1975), and a new dock, Rogers' Landing, named after the director Lynn Rogers and dedicated in 2002. In the early 1960's the camp needed more room and approached its neighbors John and Helen Morse about purchasing some of their property. The Morse family was impressed with the camp's service to children and in 1963, John and Helen Morse gave the camp 21 acres. Camp Patmos serves young people and adults who want a break from their normal lives, in a loving and caring atmosphere. In 2000 the ownership of the camp was given to the Trustees, who had been operating it from the beginning.

Hugging the roadway past the camp is a dry laid stone wall which oral histories attribute to Joseph Lincoln (c 1865). Lincoln used stones cleared from his fields to build the wall and the wall was contin-

Dry mortarless limestone wall

ued by his son and his neighbors, the Hamiltons. Similar stone walls are also found in other locations on the Island.

All the camps have made an impact on the Island. They draw children and their families from many areas to Kelleys Island for a few weeks each year. Over the years this has amounted to a lot of visitors. Many of these children campers have returned to the Island in their adult years. Their early fond memories of summer on Kelleys Island bring them back as visitors and some eventually become property owners.

Kelleys Island State Park

By 1943, the Ohio Historical Society was reviewing a proposal that would have transferred all the Kelleys Island Lime & Transport Company (KIL&T) land, almost 1,200 acres, to the State of Ohio for a purchase price of $55,000. After selling off some property, twelve years later KIL&T donated 412 acres to the Cleveland Museum of Natural History. The Scheele Preserve on Monagan Road is one of several non-contiguous parcels still owned by the Museum. Their holdings conserve some rare plant

Sand castle on Sand Beach

species. The balance of the KIL&T property was transferred to the State of Ohio in 1956, to begin the development of Kelleys Island State Park. In 1965, the State Park was composed of a boat launch, dock and 17 camp sites. Sand Beach had been a village public beach, but when the State wanted to start a park on the Island, the village transferred its beach property to the State. It is the only sand beach on the Island. Most of the other beaches are small stones or large flat shelves of limestone, and of course, are privately owned.

State Park campground attendance began with 122 visitors in 1963, 3,231 in 1964, and 12,387 in 1965. The 2006 season saw approximately 47,000 people camping at the State Park with about 180,000 visitors. The park currently is composed of 677 acres and includes the North Quarry, East Quarry, one campground, a public beach, two nature preserves and about six miles of trails. There are 129 campsites available, with 84 electrified, and two yurts, two rent-a-camps and conveniences such as flush toilets and showers.

Within the State Park, there are more than five miles of self-guided hiking trails that include beach, rocky cliff coastline, swamp, quarry, and rocky areas. In the spring, there are fields in bloom of the unusual and rare Lakeside daisy, a bright yellow daisy-like flower that seems to grow out of solid rock. It is named after Lakeside, Ohio, just across the lake from the south shore of Kelleys Island, adjacent to Marblehead, where it grows abundantly in waste quarry areas. Some daisy plants were transplanted to the Kelleys Island alvar (North Shore Preserve) in the hope that they would establish, and they have.

The North Shore Alvar deserves special mention as it is such an unusual type of environment to

Trails in the State Park cover many terrains: abandoned quarry, lakeshore, swamp, and forest. Native red cedar trees are abundant throughout the Island.

including the northern bog violet, squaw weed (an Ohio threatened plant species), and orange lichen (found nowhere else in Ohio), in addition to the Lakeside daisy.

The North Pond Nature Preserve is part of the State Park and is a 30-acre sanctuary that includes forest, marsh and a mile long board walk. It is Ohio's only state-managed "lake embayment" natural pond. Being situated in a lake coastal zone, the pond water level rises and falls with the lake level. The Preserve has younger trees, due to the de-forestation that occurred in the nineteenth century when trees were cut for steamboat fuel, but it does have a huge variety of species, and looks much like Kelleys Island must have appeared to the first humans to see it, the Native Americans. The juniper, or eastern red cedar, is abundant in the shallow limestone soil. It is a conifer that, in the fall, produces clumps of hard blue berries with a whitish bloom on them similar to that found on grapes. There are two types of dogwood, rough leaf and red-osier. Today dogwoods are the dominant species on the Island where they form dense thickets in areas that were once cleared fields and vineyards. Other trees in residence are sumac, redbud, hackberry, oak, maple, and elm, although the last two named are the least plentiful. Cottonwoods are a tall tree that spread their seed in fluffy masses in the spring. The cottony seeds collect

be found in Ohio. It is in the northwest corner of the State Park, near the shoreline. This alvar consists of open flat areas of limestone that were exposed by the glaciers. There is very little soil available, but it is home to some unusual plants

Joe Corso paints the ambience of a Kelleys Island woods.

Horseshoe Lake lies at the bottom of the abandoned east quarry area, along a State Park trail.

along edges of streets as they blow in the wind. Wild grapes spring up everywhere using trees as their trellises. Poison ivy is perhaps the most abundant plant on the Island and it grows everywhere— in the woods, fields, next to roads and sidewalks, and in home gardens. Its white berries are eaten by birds and its vegetation by deer.

Kelleys Island is on the migratory route of many bird species. The local Audubon Society hosts a week every year, usually the week after Mother's Day, timed for spring bird migration. Their program called "Nest with the Birds," features guided birding outings and speakers. The State Park trails and the North Pond Nature Preserve are great places to see much of the wildlife on Kelleys Island.

During the past ten years, over 268 species of birds have been counted, and Kelleys Island has been designated an important bird area by the National Audubon Society. Frequent sightings of bird species such as sparrows, purple martins, indigo buntings, Baltimore orioles, various warblers, black-capped chickadees, northern kingbirds, red-winged black-birds, and various waterfowl like herons, mallard and other ducks are normal. Also likely to be seen are rabbits, fox, deer, muskrat, squirrels, Lake Erie water snakes, salamanders, frogs, and turtles. State Park naturalists schedule nature and wildlife programs in the park during the peak summer months.

Community

Kelleys Island began as a township. Then in 1887, the Village of Kelleys Island incorporated and the boundaries of the new municipality included the entire land mass of the Island. Around 1834, Division Street, the first road, was established to connect the Kelleys' docks on the north and south bays. The road runs north to south and roughly cuts the island into two halves, east and west. Stores were located in various parts of the Island throughout its history, but the only continuous commercial center remains around the southern foot of Division Street. By 1900, the business district was serving 1,174 permanent residents. The community supported a doctor, barber, butcher, boot maker, and undertaker. The "downtown" included general stores, saloons, churches, a library/reading room, post office, jail and town hall.

As the north side grew in inhabitants employed in the quarry business, a community grew up there.

Monarch butterflies stop at Kelleys Island during their annual migration to Mexico.

There were rooming houses for single men, family houses and a company store. The workers came largely from Czechoslovakia (now Czech Republic and Slovakia), and Italy. Most of these structures were frame and are now gone from sight, however the remains of a community bake oven are still visible at the north end of Division Street, on present day State Park land. The south side also had quarry housing on a small short street off West Lakeshore Drive. The street runs down the middle of what is today Craft's Lakeview Cottages. The cottages themselves were once occupied by quarry workers, year-round. Craft's Lakeview Cottages are now owned by Kyle Paine, and are operated as tourist cabins.

Kelleys Island has never had a very substantial newspaper. In fact, *Kelleys Life*, the current one, is about the longest, continual, regularly published newspaper that the Island has had. From time to time people have had community newsletters, but they usually focused more on social happenings and less about news. However, a newspaper as entertainment has a long tradition. The first such text was called *The Islander*, and was published by the Kelley's Island Literary Society starting in December, 1860. Since everyone living on the Island at that time was work-

ing hard spring to fall, winter was the leisure time and coincided with publication of *The Islander*. The one published copy was as a hand-written manuscript. Members of the Society would gather every Saturday evening in the months that it was written to hear the articles read aloud, followed by discussion. Many prominent members of the community contributed to the paper, and the essays could be written on any subject. The text might be instructive like grape growing or commentaries on world events. The Literary Society was open to both men and women alike.

Because of the increase in population during the summer, Kelleys Island newspapers have shifted their publication time more towards the summer months. Most of the local papers have been small in size and short in length, with a focus on social items. The *Home Town News*, by Carol Elfers included a regular column by Coradine Myers. A paper that strove to be more topical and report political events was the *Perchie Press*, which was published by Vickie and Tim Sullivan. *Kelleys Life* is a larger format newspaper than most have been, includes advertising, and tries to include the political along with the social. It was started by John and Anne Bauswein and continues to this day, edited locally by Jacqueline Kranyak.

Downtown as painted by Joe Corso

The Lodge

Historic Downtown

In 1850, at the corner of Division and Water Street (now West Lakeshore Drive), George Kelley built a combination store and post office. The building has seen many changes in ownership and façade, but is still operated as a business and remains the oldest commercial structure on the Island. An 1888 guide book describes it as "the headquarters for the whole Island, rich and poor alike." People would come to collect their mail, buy groceries, and socialize. A group of island men spent their winter leisure time playing checkers there. They were known as "The Independent Order of Island Loafers" which somehow was shortened to "The Lodge."

The Matso family owned and operated the restaurant-bar for two generations, first by Joseph Matso and then by his son Russell Matso. The original frame building was re-surfaced in brick by Ed and Fran Kuchar when they operated it as The Water St. Cafe. The commercial space has been used mainly as successive restaurant-bars for many years, and in 2006 was purchased by Ted and Lisa Klonaris and re-named The Captain's Corner.

In 1877 The Island House, situated on the northeast corner of Division and Water Streets, caught fire and burned to the ground. As the hotel was burning, Islanders formed a bucket brigade to bring water up from the lake which they threw on buildings across Division Street from the hotel. This saved the downtown business district from total destruction.

Next to "The Lodge" on Water Street (now West Lakeshore Drive) is the Village Pump, built in 1890 to house the Post Office. The two story structure has held a barber shop, confectionary, social hall, and doctor's office. After Prohibition, Charles Martin added a third story for living quarters and opened a bar on the main street level. One side was a restaurant-bar and the other side an ice cream parlor for many years. It became a favorite gathering place for Islanders and continues that tradition today as the Village Pump.

Town Hall

On Division Street, in 1861, Datus and Sara Dean Kelley had built what is now known as the town hall, as a gift to the community. Kelley Hall, as it was formally named on its face, was "dedicated to truth" and was open to "every creed and doctrine." During the early years, various religious denominations used the hall before they erected their own buildings. It was also used by many organizations, the "Lyceum" literary society, drama club, brass band, and choral society.

Kelley Hall

The Hall is located in the downtown central commercial district. Constructed of native limestone with wood trim, the town hall was the first public building on Kelleys Island. The Ohio Historical Society classifies the architecture of the town hall as vernacular with Greek Revival and Gothic elements. Vernacular is a term used to describe architectural construction and alterations of style that reflect local popular taste or limitations of local resources, for example, materials and workmanship. The use of local materials is also a demonstration of thrift and practicality. The popularity of classic revival styles was generated during the latter half of the eighteenth century to the mid-nineteenth century by the discovery and subsequent interest in the ancient ruins of Greece. At the time, there were many books published and lectures given about the antiquities that archaeologists were discovering. With the general interest of the western world in this archeological work came an appreciation of the classical styles of architecture.

Americans were captivated by these styles which recalled the grandeur and beauty of far-away places and long ago. The revival styles drew their inspiration from Europe and became Americanized on the East Coast. The classic revival styles spread easily through builder's pattern books, and through the training of architects. They reached the Sandusky/Kelleys Island area not long after their east coast debut. American architects used Greek architectural elements and applied them to modern, practical plans. Greek Revival and Early Gothic Revival reached their zenith around 1820-1860, coinciding with the early development of Kelleys Island. Kelleys town hall is a Greek Revival structure interpreted in limestone, a local material. In general, limestone was a favorite material for most large public buildings that were erected before and after the Civil War and limestone was a plentiful, readily available building material on Kelleys Island.

Originally the town hall was a block shape, like most Greek Revival buildings. It did not have the current front entrance, or the doctor's office entrance, nor did it have the stage to the east with its accompanying irregular rear wall. The Hall has traditionally been used for many civic activities. School graduations were held in the town hall until the recent gymnasium addition to Estes school. By the mid-twentieth century, stripes were added to the floor along with other accoutrements so that school children and adults could use the hall for sports activities. In the nineteenth and early twentieth centuries, the building was used for public gatherings, plays, dinner dances, and musical programs. It is still used for such events, but today there are fewer of them. The Island Singers, a summer group, puts on a musical show at the end of the tourist season, and Santa Claus always arrives at the Christmas Community Potluck to hand out gifts to the Island's children. The Village Council holds its meetings in the hall and the Chamber of Commerce holds a Welcome Back Fish Fry at the beginning of the tourist season and hosts a holiday boutique in the hall over Thanksgiving week-end. Kelleys town hall continues to be the center of community activity in the twenty-first century just as it had been in the nineteenth.

Farms

Islanders had to be very self-reliant. In the winter, when the lake froze, the usual shipping transportation was finished. If the lake created ice thick enough, people and animals could travel on its surface, although this was always dangerous and unpredictable.

Several farmers had dairy cows, but the best preserved barn, on Woodford Road, belonged to George Becker. When the barn and milk bottling plant were built about 1917, it was one of the most modern in the region. Becker operated the Island's largest dairy into the 1940's, with a herd of more than twenty Jersey milk cows. Becker's milk, butter, and cheese products were marketed under the name "Island Jersey Farms." Dry (mortarless) limestone walls that marked some of Becker's pasture boundaries are still visible along Woodford Road. The Becker barn also demonstrates one of the differences in farms on the Island from the mainland, most of the barns were painted white instead of red, the more prevalent color in the rest of Ohio.

Becker Barn, Woodford Road

Henry Trieschman was the Island butcher. He emigrated from Hesse, Germany, prior to 1870. His frame house is still standing across from the Becker House and barn on Woodford Road. His slaughterhouse was located just east of the Becker farm property. For three generations the Trieschman family operated a meat market near the corner of Division and Water Streets. Trieschman had 35 acres

Former Trieschman House, Division Street

of pasture along Woodford and Monagan Roads and purchased his cattle on the mainland. Cattle were brought to the Island by boat or by herding them across thick ice in the winter.

Walter Brown had a farm on the corner of Woodford Road and present day Harbor Lane. He had milk cows, chickens, and in some years specialty crops like turkeys. Some of the farm products went to the store that he owned with Frank Lange on Division Street, next to the downtown park. The Lange and Brown General Store (c 1929) later became Brown's General Store and was very active up to the 1960's. Along with the Island Market, owned by Franklin and Laura Jean Pohorence, the stores provided groceries for year round Islanders as well as summer people and tourists. The building that was Brown's General Store still stands today and is operated by Cindy Holmes as The General Store with items for tourists, although it's traditional white exterior has been replaced by a treated red wood. The Island Market is now owned by Rob and Kim Watkins, and the location has been in continuous operation as a market since the 1860's. Kim Watkins served for many years as an E.M.T. and has also been elected to the school board.

Home Life

A little should be said about the experience of families when Kelleys Island had a large year-round population, before and a little after 1900. Since they were living on an island, cut off from larger cities, families had to be quite self-sufficient in all respects. Women canned the fruits and vegetables from their gardens, and made their own jam and jellies out of crabapples, grapes, and quinces. They made bread and their own cookies and cakes. Milk came from their own cow or a local farmer's, and of course, it was not pasteurized or homogenized. Butter was produced from the cream. Lard was the most prevalent shortening. Eggs came from their own chickens or a local farmer's. Cattle were raised and slaughtered locally, and the meat was sold at Trieschman's Meat Market. In a family, the women made the food for the table every day and for special occasions. They hand beat 12 egg whites when they wanted to make angel food cake.

Families were large, typically with many children, six to twelve, and sometimes multi-generational. Wives washed their husband's and children's clothes on a washboard, heating water on their wood or kerosene cook stoves, and hanging the clothes outside on a wash line to dry. Women got together during the slower parts of the year (not the growing season) to make quilts on large frames. They sewed clothes on treadle sewing machines, and knit and crocheted both clothes and pretty edges on linens. If there were children, then life was continually busy and tiring.

Children walked to the school closest to their home. Fun was playing with a few toys, and with other neighborhood children. In the summer there was swimming in the lake; in the winter there was ice skating and sledding. Only outhouses were in service and water came from hand pumps and cisterns. Instead of electricity, most families had gasoline or oil lamps with glass chimneys that had to be cleaned every day. When weather permitted, many times the men took a bath at the lakeshore or in quarry pools.

People consulted home medical books about their ailments, especially if it was during one of the too frequent periods when the Island was without a doctor. Men split wood and got coal from the Store Dock (the store building on the dock just west of the Casino) for the winter. There would likely be music at home, music made on pianos and violins, and in choral groups and churches. Neighbors visited each other on Sunday. There was time to talk and there were stories to be told. Baseball was very popular and remained so through the first half of the twentieth century. The teams traveled to play other teams both from the Lake Erie Islands and mainland towns. The Island also had several brass bands. Men played instruments in bands that were always ready for community events such as marches on holidays. After work in fishing, farming, and quarrying, the men stopped by the local bar for a beer before going home for supper. Much of the family social life revolved around the churches. Especially noted within the community were the beginnings and ends of lives, when all the community would join with a family in its joy or sorrow. Life was hard and required much from everyone.

In the downtown park, once the site of the burned ruins of the Island House Hotel, stands a monument to the soldiers from Kelleys Island that have fought in the Spanish American War, the Civil War, and World War I and II. The names of those lost in battle are inscribed on the face of the monument. The Island has a long tradition of patriotism and military service which in 2006 finds Islanders and members of Island families still serving. Islanders have remained thankful to the members of the armed services for their service to country and community. Each Memorial Day there is a crowd at the cemetery gathered to remember and honor those who served in the armed forces. The older more luxurious day-long celebrations of the 1930's have been replaced by shorter but meaningful programs guided by V.F.W. Post 9908. The long tradition of service to country continues with islanders Michael and Violet Feyedelem's son. In 2006, Commander Michael S. Feyedelem, on staff with the Joint Chiefs of Staff at the Pentagon, gave the Memorial Day address.

Quarrying

On the north side of the Island, in 1833, according to old records, John Clemens was the first man to quarry limestone. It was the beginning of a lucrative business and by the 1870's there were small quarry operations all over the Island. The north quarry stone was Upper Helderberg or Columbus limestone, which often lay close to the surface in four distinct layers. The top layer was about four feet of a bluish stone known as extra cap rock, then about nine feet of bluish grey cap rock, followed by six feet of building stone, and deepest

was a layer of lighter grey bottom rock which extended to below the level of the lake. The inferior extra cap rock was crushed for road building. The cap rock was used for flux. The bottom layer of rock was used for lime burning and the building stone layer was either burned to make lime or sold as blocks for building. From 1886 to 1935 the Kelleys Island Lime & Transport Co. (KIL&T) quarried limestone on Kelleys Island on their 1500 acres, having consolidated the previous small independent quarries.

KIL&T had purchased the Norman Kelley and Company quarries and as the wine industry became less profitable and land prices fell, quarrying once again became a major growth industry. The stone has been used in many Detroit and Michigan churches, office buildings in Cleveland, Ohio, and the Poe lock at Sault Saint Marie. In the 1800's the Quarry advertised in Europe for workers to come to Kelleys Island for opportunity. As new workers came from Ireland, Italy, and Eastern Europe, the ethnic mix of the Island changed. The Island had been settled by German immigrants who were attracted to Kelleys Island because of work in the wine industry. As many of the winery jobs were eliminated due to economics, many of the Germans also started to work in the quarries.

The first railroad for the quarry industry was built around 1854 to haul stone to a south side dock. It was only 500 feet long. It operated by gravity on the outbound trip, and used horses for the return trip to haul the empty cars back to the upland quarry site. By 1900, there were 16 lime kilns operating at the north side quarry, with 500 men and 50 horses working in kiln areas, quarries, cooper's shop, and docks. The daily capacity was fifty-six tons. After 1898, stone was hauled from the quarry site on narrow-gauge movable rails by Shay engines. The Shay engine was invented by Ephraim Shay of Harbor Springs, Michigan, in the late nineteenth century. Designed especially for the logging and mining industries, the majority continued to be built in Lima, Ohio, well into the first half of the twentieth century. The engine was distinguished from the usual locomotive in that it was built with a flexible frame which allowed it to traverse uneven track without jumping off the track. The Shay engine was also the first geared locomotive which gave it the power to

Lime-kills north side about 1902

pull heavy loads up steep grades at a slow speed along narrow, sharp curves. The Kelleys Island Lime & Transport Co. was reputed to have purchased thirty five Shay engines from 1898 to 1923, more than any other company in the world. The quarry company (KIL&T) expanded into a conglomerate with operations in five states and a fleet of its own ships.

Limestone ranked among the top five commodities in tonnage in shipping on the Great Lakes. In 1910, KIL&T constructed a new loading dock on the west side, at the spot currently known as West Bay Inn, and the company increased the volume of stone shipped. By 1912, KIL&T shipped 546,922 tons on 459 boats. The peak of production was reached in 1923 when 576,980 tons were shipped. Around that time records show that the Island had grown to a population of 1200, with a library and a high school.

During the Great Depression of the 1930's the building stone market went through drastic changes. At the same time, the better grades of stone found on the Island had been mostly depleted. The quarrying moved east of Division Street where the top surface limestone was good for use in building roads and as

flux stone. Much of the railroad equipment was cut up and sold as scrap metal, although remnants of some of the rails can still be found in the State Park old quarry area, along with cinders on the ground, from the days that burning coal drove the little Shay

The State Park trail on the east end of Ward Road le to one of the abandoned quarry areas.

The Lafarge quarry produces over 1,000,000 tons of stone annually from Kelleys Island.

View of quarry from road

engines. When Kelleys Island Lime & Transport closed the quarry in the fall of 1940, with the last shipments leaving the Island in 1941, the decrease in employment caused the population to decline to 275 people. Many second and third generation Island families were forced to leave the Island to find employment elsewhere. During this period the available Island jobs were in fishing and farming, which also ended within the next two decades.

The West Bay area has continued to be quarried intermittently from the 1960's to present day, by several different companies, but under the same name of Kellstone. Mr. Breckling operated the quarry and then sold it to the Levy Company in Michigan. They operated it for a while, and then closed it for a number of years before selling it to James Palladino in 1989 who continued operation under the same name, Kellstone, Inc.

After purchasing the property, Palladino began renovating it to begin quarrying again. The loading dock at West Bay was partially dismantled and was eventually dynamited in 1989, to make room for more modern equipment. After installing the latest technology, the company shipped more crushed stone in a day than could have been produced during weeks of hand labor in earlier times. Various grades of stone have been quarried, crushed, and shipped to Cleveland docks for use as base material for road building and in making asphalt. The north side and east quarries were never re-opened and today are incorporated into the Kelleys Island State Park, part of the State of Ohio Park system.

Lafarge, an international company with headquarters in Paris, France, purchased the quarry business in March 2004. Lafarge also works the Marblehead quarry located on the mainland directly south of Kelleys Island. The loading dock at Marblehead can be easily seen from the south shore of Kelleys Island where large freighters from Canada and the United States regularly load stone. Lafarge operates the Kelleys Island Quarry for eight months a year, April through November. Many of the quarry workers come on the ferry in the morning and return to the mainland every afternoon. Gone are the days when the Island could supply all the people needed for the total work force. Lafarge Kelleys Island Quarry employs about 18 people to produce one million tons of base stone annually. In 2006, the quarry is mining stone from the Detroit River Group formation of limestone. This layer has fossils throughout it and especially in the lower bands of stone. Pockets of minerals such as calcite, barite, and fluorite are sometimes found. The majority of the one million tons of stone mined annually is sent by barge to the Cleveland, Ohio market for use as construction aggregate.

Lafarge updated some of the equipment and has automated the plant and load out system. The plant is operating at 800 tons per hour of product on the conveyor. The average load out is 2000 tons per hour and is accomplished in about 5 hours time. Throughout the summer months, the blasting can be heard both from the Kelleys Island quarry and from the Marblehead quarry. About 20,000 tons of stone are moved per blast on the Island. Lafarge, as a large international company, brings with it greater resources than the quarry business has seen in the past when it was run by independent businessmen. Lafarge has an excellent safety record and conserves on its use of electricity with a transfer switch that allows the plant to run on its own generator part of the time. In 2004 Lafarge Kelleys Island Quarry was given an award for site improvement and became part of a progressive awards system with the National Stone Sand and Gravel Association. As a public service, the quarry hosted an open house for Islanders to see the operation.

In 2005 Lafarge began working with the Wildlife Habitat Council to manage the unused land in an ecologically sensitive manner to benefit local wildlife. Plans include bird houses for the Eastern Bluebird to re-establish them on the Island, nesting places for robins, and bee boxes. Brush piles for rabbit and other small wildlife protection and raptor perches are included in the plan, along with the planting of switch grass and wildflowers, including Lakeside daisy beds. Killdeer regularly nest on the floor of the quarry and fox, coyote, and deer frequent the area. The wildlife habitat is created through volunteer work by employees. In 2006, Lafarge received Wildlife Habitat Council certification and a Showplace award from National Stone Sand and Gravel Association. Once established, Lafarge has agreed to maintain and monitor the wildlife habitat and plans to eventually have an area accessible by the public to view it.

As quarries were opened in different places on Kelleys Island over the years, a variety of stone was encountered. Much of the building quality stone was quarried many years ago and although most of the stone is used for road base today, some building quality stone still remains to be quarried if the market for it revives. While the foundations of many of the older homes on the Island, and some houses and other buildings are built entirely of Island limestone (like the German Reformed Church- now home to the Kelleys Island Historical Association and the town hall on Division Street), the principal use locally for stone today is also for road beds and driveways. This limestone makes the characteristic cloud of white lime dust as it is traversed by vehicles. The Village of Kelleys Island also uses fine stone particles, called screenings, rather than salt on the roads during the winter months.

Immigrants

Much of Kelleys Island was settled by immigrants from Europe. The largest group came from Germany and worked in the winery business. Some purchased land and grew their own grapes, and some worked as laborers in the vineyards. In 1900, the Island was covered in grapes, small farms, and quarries. German was spoken in many of the immigrant's homes, socially and at church. There were other ethnic communities on the north side where the quarry housing, store, and headquarters stood. Today only two houses are left standing from the quarry workers' community, off Bookerman Road, at the entrance to the Village Transfer Station. This area was at one time a bustling community where Italian, Czech, and Slovak languages were overheard.

Kelleys Island Lime & Transport Co. needed workers and they sent emissaries and publicity to towns in Europe to obtain them. The immigrants responded to advertisements for men to work in the quarry industry. Some men came alone and some came with their families. At one time there were five neighborhood stores dotted around the Island, each serving its own small community.

New immigrants brought new religions to the Island. At one time there were five churches, an Orthodox for some of the Slovaks, a Roman Catholic, a German Reformed, a Protestant, and a Congregational. The location of the Orthodox Church is marked by a double cross of the Eastern Rites on Division Street, towards the center of the

Ice boats and skate sails on the east end

Zion United Methodist Church, watercolor by Leon Heinl.

St. Michael Roman Catholic Church on Chapel Street at Addison Street.

The Congregational Church was on Division Street near Chapel Street. When the church was razed, wood from it was used to construct the east wall classroom addition to Zion United Methodist Church.

St. Michael Roman Catholic Church in spring.

Island. The church was razed around 1943, and the wood from it was used to construct a private home. The Congregational Church was razed, and some of the wood was used to build the social hall addition to the Zion United Methodist Church. The German Reformed Church became the Kelleys Island Historical Association.

Still in use today are the St. Michael Roman Catholic, and the Zion United Methodist Churches. Both have regular services throughout the year and both are served by clergy that do not live on the Island. In the summer, both churches have summer Bible school. When the population dropped severely throughout the mid twentieth century, the Island lost its permanent resident clergy. Both active churches are served by clergy that fly to the Island to give services every week.

Isolation

In the nineteenth and early twentieth centuries, the Island was pretty well isolated during the winter months. Once ice began to form in the lake, shipping and all boat traffic would stop. When the ice became thick enough, six inches or more, people traveled over it. In the nineteenth century horses and foot power were the common transportation methods. After automobiles were more prevalent and people had "old" cars available, the doors and the tops were removed so they could be used for travel across the ice. Removal of some of the car parts made the cars a little lighter on the ice, but more importantly, it was easier to jump out if the car broke through the ice. Many cars still lay at the bottom of Lake Erie between Kelleys Island and Marblehead, along with a few snow mobiles from the latter half of the twentieth century.

Before television and computers, the residents had to make their own fun. There were a number of bands on the Island, and there was a play at least once a year where the community's adults were the actors. There were also men's and women's groups that would socialize, like the German Reformed Church Ladies Aid, the Maccabees, the Knights of St. John and its Auxiliary, and the Odd Fellows. The Elfers store on Division Street sold dry goods, and women made clothes for their families on treadle sewing machines or went to the local dressmaker. Fancy wedding cakes were made locally.

For seventeen years a publication known as *The Islander* was written by the Kelley's Island Literary Society during the winter months, starting in December 1860. The members contributed the essays. The membership included W. Webb, Bristol, A. Kelley, F. Kelley, and M. Ward. One copy was made, written in long-hand and then read at "The Lodge" once a week, on Saturday evening.

Autumn signaled the return of winter. It was the time for canning home grown produce to be used during the winter months when fresh vegetables were not available. Once the boats stopped, in November, it was difficult to obtain much variety in food. Homes had pantries that were well stocked for the winter. Today Islanders still stock their houses with goods, especially paper products and frozen items, before winter locks the Island in a frozen sea.

Winter months still bring isolation. Travel is difficult and expensive. Often travel plans must be changed due to the weather. Islanders are aware of the wind year-round. Erie is the shallowest of the Great Lakes and has a reputation for being treacherous because storms quickly affect the lake surface. Strong winds actually move the body of water in the lake. Depending on the force and direction of the wind, the water rises and almost covers docks, or is pushed away from shore, leaving boats resting on the lake bed. A strong west wind can send the water out of the Toledo basin to Buffalo. A strong north or south wind can leave either the Marblehead dock or the Kelleys Island dock without enough water to dock the ferry.

Doctoring

The Island had resident doctors intermittently, but has never had a hospital. Some years there would be a trained nurse on the Island, but until about 1940, when children were being born at home, one of the "practical nurses", Laura Hughes or Rose Dwelle, was called. Although neither woman had formal nurses' training, she helped the doctor deliver the baby and then would stay in the house after the birth to cook for the family and help the mother and newborn. Doctors were actively sought by the Village government and were paid a stipend from the Village to augment their income. After the one steady doctor became semi-retired, the last decades of the twentieth century saw some attempts by the Village at opening a clinic and trying to attract another doctor at least part-time, but nothing became a permanent solution. Through an arrangement that the Village Council made with St. Vincents/University Medical Center/St. Rita's Life Flight in Toledo, a life flight helicopter is available and a paramedic is resident on the Island most of the time. Also a small group of dedicated individuals trains and volunteers as Emergency Medical Technicians.

The last medical doctor to service the Island was Dr. Heinz Boker, an Islander for most of his life. He was born in Germany and moved to Kelleys Island with his family at age six, not speaking any English. He is a great American success story. Being bright and willing to work hard, he graduated from the Kelleys Island School and then studied Chemical Engineering, obtaining a Bachelor's degree at Ohio State University. He was employed by Battelle Institute for a few years before returning to Columbus to enter medical school. After becoming a medical doctor he joined the U.S. Army. He returned from military service and began his career as the doctor serving the Lake Erie Islands, using his own plane to get from one island to another. For many years he volunteered four weeks annually to work at Iowa Indian Reservations and in Central and South American countries to make medical care available to those with scarce resources. When in semi-retirement, he returned to Kelleys Island and remained the medical doctor for Islanders until health forced him into complete retirement. He was an exceptional family doctor, visiting his patients every day if necessary, demonstrating the kind of care and supervision no longer found in most of the "civilized" world. Dr. Boker's and his wife Kathryn's generosity to the Island and its people was also demonstrated when they gave property to the Village to expand the airport.

Since the passing of Dr. Boker in 2003, there has been no doctor available on the Island. Residents must go by boat or plane to the mainland for medical care. There are periods during every year, usually at the turn of seasons, when there is no transportation to or from the Island—especially when there is ice in the lake and fog in the air. Those times make one pause and think about earlier times and how people lived and died, sometimes at the turn of a hat.

For a number of years in the early twentieth century there was a mortician, William Burger, who provided full funeral service including a hearse.

Until at least the 1930's, a wreath was put on the front door to mark the home of the deceased. Burger lived on the south shore, today's West Lakeshore Drive. His mortician's work was performed in a building behind his house. The corpse would then be taken back to the deceased's home for visitation. Burger's work shop was renovated into living space by the present owners. Both buildings, workshop and home, are owned by the Zettler family who operated the original Burger house, in front, as tourist accommodations.

There were not many cars on the Island until the 1950's. Before then, children and adults walked, which limited the distance they would go in their daily lives. The Island still functioned more or less as neighborhoods. Since the Island was all farms and vineyards, the closest neighbor was usually down the road a bit. This made Island families self-reliant and the physical isolation of an island also made Islanders interdependent. Everyone knew everything about everybody. In the midst of this close knit society, individuals could still be quite private about personal aspects of their lives.

Attitudes and social behavior in the core society changed greatly by the mid twentieth century with the influx of residents that were raised on the mainland and the exodus of older Island families that were forced to seek work off the Island. Newer residents brought with them more variety of social and life experiences than was possible for the traditional Island family, and the melding of the old and the new created a different community. Another aspect that has changed is accent. Prior to about 1950, the Islanders had an accent that was the same as southern Canada, just to the north. Talking to someone from Pelee Island sounded a lot like speaking with a Kelley Islander. The combination of changes in the accent of Sanduskians after WW II and the new mainland arrivals to the Island, have altered the once distinctive verbal patterns. Kelleys Island now mirrors the American mix of speaking sounds for the upper mid-west region.

Schools

Most of the teachers came to Kelleys Island from the mainland. It has always been a place of many first year teachers. After a year or two, most of them find a job elsewhere and move away, making room for another young teacher. One of the notable teachers that stayed was Jessie Abbott who came from southern Ohio in 1945, as a young woman on her first teaching job. She fell in love with a local man, Charles Martin Jr. They married and raised their family on the Island. Jessie Martin went on to become an author, writing several books about Kelleys Island life and also books about her early experiences in southern Ohio. Charles Martin, Jr., known as "Jakie" is a fourth generation Kelley Islander. He was a builder and a farmer, and sold real estate on the Island. He purchased 92 acres from the Becker family, part of which he developed into a subdivision at Hamilton's Point (east end of Woodford Road, north side).

Estes school

Lillian Mallory came as a teacher around 1940 and married an Island man Lynn Brown. Lillian Brown taught music at school and gave music lessons from her home, as well as leading community choral groups. The most recent young teacher to succumb to the romance of an Island man was Patricia Greeney, who married James Seeholzer. James Seeholzer was the descendant of an old Island family, and he had a construction and excavating business on the Island. Jim and Pat raised their family on the Island, and Pat Seeholzer continued to be part of the Kelleys Island school system until her retirement in 2006, after forty years of teaching Island children.

Other local teachers were Helen Marchky, Evangeline Bonchi, Alice Beatty, Nadine (Bickley) Brown, Hazel Lange, Kathleen Lange, Dorothy Jean Schlesselman and Kurt Boker. Kurt Boker, a younger brother of Dr. Heinz Boker, graduated from Kelleys Island High School in 1938. In 1941 he was drafted into the U.S. Army about a month before Pearl Harbor. In the Army he worked on the ALCAN Highway (Alaska-Canada) with the 35th Construction Engineers and later served with the 35th Combat Engineers at the Battle of the Bulge in Europe. He was discharged in 1945 and returned to Kelleys Island, working at Minshall's vineyards and orchards on the northwest of the Island until he entered Ohio State University, to study painting and sculpture in the Fine Arts Department. He changed his major to geology and obtained a Bachelor's Degree, after which he did graduate study. There was an opening for a school teacher on Kelleys Island and Kurt Boker returned to accept it in 1956. He studied every summer until he obtained his teaching degree and certification. After two years he was appointed the Executive Head of the school, then Administrative Assistant, in which position he remained until his retirement in 1982.

Kurt Boker's teaching style was innovative for its time and for many years he expanded class outside the school room, teaching history and science through field trips around the Island. The north woods, open fields, quarries and shoreline offered students a learning experience in the natural sciences through research and discovery of local flora and fauna. A rare Marbled Salamander about six inches long was discovered during one of the student outdoor classes. It is black with white or yellow markings. During these class trips, fossils were examined, geology was illustrated, and students were educated in the Island's history.

Mr. Boker retired on the Island after his work in education and continued to do extensive research, chronicling Island history and the genealogy of Island families. Before this book went to press, Kurt E. Boker passed from this life at the age of 86. He had lived on the Island from age 4 to his death. Always inquisitive, he researched many aspects of local natural history and the genealogy of Island families. He gave his extensive research to the Sandusky Library and copies of many of the manuscripts are available in the Kelleys Island Branch library. Kurt Boker was the recognized Island historian and the person to whom all other historians went to have their questions answered.

Ironclad mail boat on south shore

Mail

One of the aspects of contemporary life that we now take for granted is the ease of communication between people both for pleasure and business. Families today are more likely to e-mail or phone each other than write a letter.

During the early settlement of Kelleys Island, before phones and electronic mail, even receiving a letter was difficult. Sometime shortly after the Kelleys came, a sailboat named the *Humming Bird* was used to carry passengers and mail between Sandusky and the Island. This was about a dozen years before the first official post office was established on the Island. During this un-official mail era letters would be addressed such as:

> Mr. Datus Kelley
> Kelleys Island
> Sandusky, Ohio

The mail was kept in the Sandusky Post Office until either someone called in person for it, or an agent picked up the mail for transport to the Island. Letters from the Island were brought to the Sandusky Post Office for mailing. Eventually, during the navigation season, two steamboats, the *Islander* and the *Island Queen*, were used to transport mail, along with passengers and supplies.

The first Post Office was in "The Lodge", the building still standing on the corner of Division Street and West Lakeshore Drive, now a restaurant/bar. The first four Postmasters were George Kelley, appointed 5-13-1852; Wm. S. Webb, appointed 6-3-1854; Alfred S. Kelley, appointed 2-6-1868; and Erastus Huntington, appointed 2-6-1872.

Between 1851 and 1860, envelopes were produced with the imprint of a map of Kelleys Island in the upper left corner. At least eight known examples are in private philatelic collections.

During the winter months, mail had to come over the ice. The mail came on a small open boat called the iron-clad, named for the iron strips that were added to the exterior. Ice can be very hard and destructive to a wooden hull. The mail, and maybe a passenger, would come over the ice daily in good weather and sometimes once in two weeks during poor weather. The trip could be difficult and take at least several hours. The boat, with runners attached to the bottom of the hull, had to be hauled and pushed over ice and slush, and when open water was encountered, the boat handlers had to use paddles to row. The Postmaster had a telescope at the Post Office from which he watched for the approach of the mail boat. When it was sighted, word spread and townspeople came to the lakefront to help haul the boat up onto the land. The mail was then sorted and distributed. It is recorded that the mail boat was never lost.

Today the mail comes by plane once a day, except for a few summer months when it arrives twice a day. When the weather is too bad to fly, there is no mail. When the mail does arrive, after giving the Postmaster just enough time to sort it, the members of the community begin to come to the Post Office to retrieve their correspondence. During the winter months the Post Office becomes a community meeting place. Many Islanders seem to arrive there at about the same time each day, when they can greet each other and catch up on the news.

Airplanes

Kelleys Island owes a lot to an early aviation pioneer, Milton Hersberger. He was born in Anderson, Indiana, where he learned to fly, working as a pilot's helper in exchange for flying lessons. He was a barnstormer, and became a test pilot and managed airports in Chicago, Youngstown, and Sandusky. He flew a plane for Parker Brothers, in Sandusky, and in February, 1929, he flew one passenger, to an adjacent island, Put-In-Bay on South Bass Island. The sole passenger was Father Maerder, the priest that served both Kelleys Island and Put-In-Bay. This was an unusual event for the small village of Put-In-Bay, and school was dismissed so that the children could watch the plane land. Evidently Hersberger was favorably impressed by this greeting

Mail plane

Bi-plane

and after the flight, he organized his own company, Erie Isle Airways. It started with 50 acres of land on Put-In-Bay for his airport, which he purchased with his life savings. The superstructure of the hangar was brought to Put-In-Bay across the ice from Kelleys Island one winter.

Hersberger later acquired the Port Clinton Airport and started daily trips. On November 11, 1930, he made his first commercial flight with his first passenger in a three-place Waco biplane. He helped Kelleys Island's mail carrier during difficult icy conditions and was eventually rewarded with a year-round contract for U.S. mail service by air to all of the United States Lake Erie islands. Hersberger was flying a Standard Biplane in May, 1934, when the engine blew apart over the lake near Lakeside. Hersberger and seven bags of mail landed in the water. A commercial fish boat saw him and came to his rescue. Will Haas, the Put-In-Bay telegraph operator for fifty years, offered Hersberger the money necessary to purchase his first Tri-Motor plane. He

Tri-motor

would eventually own seven of them. He owned five Tri-Motors by 1935 and at that time he changed the name of his company to Island Airways.

Hersberger and his "Tin Goose", as the Ford Tri-Motor was affectionately called, were the lifeline of the Lake Erie islands for many years. The planes carried the U.S. Mail, passengers, supplies, the clergy, doctors, pets, the ill, and also the dead. In the 1940's the Tin Goose flew twice daily to Kelleys Island, in the morning with the mail and a second flight in the afternoon. The first airport on Kelleys Island was at the corner of Monagan and Hamilton Roads, in what is now the Travel Air Taxi Inc. Subdivision, on land leased by Hersberger.

In August, 1953, Hersberger, who was by this time an Island legend, sold his airline to Ralph Dietrick from Sandusky. While Hersberger lived to be 85 years old, it is said that he never again set foot in his Port Clinton Airport, nor piloted a plane. The corporate title of the business was changed to Sky Tours, Inc., and the name of Island Airways became Island Airlines. Dietrick expanded the business and was soon operating out of both Sandusky and Port Clinton airports with a fleet of Ford Tri-Motors.

In 1962, Dietrick sold his Sandusky airport to Sue and Harry Griffing, while he continued to fly primarily between Port Clinton and the Bass Islands, leaving Kelleys Island service to the Griffing family. Harry Griffing was an aviation pioneer in the Sandusky area. From 1937 to 1946 he operated the Sandusky Airport. He and his wife T. Sue Griffing were both pilots. They purchased land on Columbus Avenue, south of Strub Road in Sandusky for their first airport named Griffing Flying Services, which they held until 1962, when they bought property off Route 6 in Sandusky for the current Griffing Sandusky Airport. T. Sue Griffing passed away in 1990, and Harry Griffing in 2001, leaving their business for their children to continue. Son H. Thomas, Jr. is a pilot for the airline as is his son Thomas. Daughter Melodie (Griffing) Taylor also works in the family business.

The airport in use today, the Kelleys Island Municipal Airport, is along Monagan Road, to the southeast of the site of the first airport. It is owned and operated by the Village of Kelleys Island. In 1948, the village decided that it wanted a new municipal airport and started arranging for land.

The Island had quite a few local pilots for the size of the community, probably because of the ease of transportation that a plane afforded to people living on an island, and they wanted a municipal airport. The Chamber of Commerce and V.F.W. Post 9908 supported and contributed to the creation of the airport. Walter "Sonnee" Elfers organized the volunteers who actually built the airport runway. Men worked during the day, many as fishermen, and spent their spare time hauling stone and running equipment. Breckling, a Cleveland firm, operated the quarry at the time, and Robert Overcasher remembered that the local men hauled screenings from the quarry, some loaded by hand, into their own trucks to take to the site. Then they put calcium chloride on the screenings to make a hard surface for the runway. Many local men worked on the airport for over a year, all volunteering their time and their equipment: Sonnee Elfers, Floyd, Donald, and Roy Erne, Ollie Schlesselman, Bob Overcasher, Robert Schnittker, Henry Beatty and Jay Norris—to name a few. Jay Norris, councilman, was asked by Mayor Beltz to arrange for a bulldozer and volunteers to finish work at the airport in early December, 1949, and it was formally dedicated shortly thereafter, with approximately 140 private planes flying in for the celebration. Henry Beatty became mayor on January 1, 1950 and continued the airport development. In the winter, the airport is the lifeline to the Island, providing transportation for persons and merchandise when the lake navigation season ends, until it resumes in late spring.

Dr. Heinz Boker, himself once a pilot, owned property adjacent to the airport. In 2000, he and his wife Kathryn Boker gave a substantial amount of their holdings to the village for use as airport expansion. At this point in time the airport has two runways, the original east west runway and a newer north south runway. Future development plans for the airport continue.

Boats and Ferries

The first recorded service between the Lake Erie islands and Sandusky was in 1846, made by the *Islander*. In 1854 she was succeeded by the *Comet*. The *Island Queen* ran between 1855 and 1866. Following those, there has been a succession of boats: *Evening Star* (1866 to 1973); *Eighth Ohio*

(1868-1869); *Reindeer* (1869-1873); *B.F. Ferris* (1872-1889), *Gazelle* (1973-1888); *Golden Eagle* (1874-1880); *Jay Cooke* (1880-1888 and 1901-1903); *City of Sandusky*, (1888-1894); *Arrow* (1895-1922); *Chippewa* (1923-1938); and the steamer *City of Hancock* (1939).

The *Walk-in-the-Water* was the first steamboat on Lake Erie. She made stops at Kelleys Island on her east-west run between Buffalo and Detroit, but more frequently she stopped at Sandusky. The *Arrow* serviced the Island from 1895 until it burned in 1922. The *Messenger* started Island service in 1922 and ran until 1946. The *Chippewa* started in 1923 and had its last regular service in 1938. In 1929 the *Tourist* ran to Kelleys Island. The *Erie Isle* ran the pre-tourist season route and had Sunday moonlight cruises from Sandusky to Kelleys Island in 1931, and continued in service off an on through 1939.

The *Welcome* ran for a short time 1950-51 in competition with Neuman Boat Line. It was an oil-burning auto ferry, owned by Islanders Frank "Chick" Hamilton and Irma Conkle. "Chick" Hamilton was the boat pilot. It ran from the Bickley Dock in Sandusky to the Store Dock, which was located at the foot of Division Street on the south side of the Island. Today the dock still juts out immediately to the west of the Casino Restaurant, and still hosts tourist boats. The large store that stood for many years on the dock and was the center of the downtown business and boat travel, is gone.

Regular ferry service is a very important item to people who live on an island. Boats provide the transportation during the majority of each year for both tourists and Islanders. From about the mid-1950's onward flat top car ferries have been in use, which allow people to drive their own cars on and off the ferry quickly. They are perfect for the tourist industry. They carry more cars than the older bow shaped boats that sometimes had to have the boat crew manage the cars on and off the ferry. The flat-top ferry proved to be so efficient that it is the only type in use today.

Neuman Boat Line

When John P. Neuman of Sandusky began the Neuman Boat Line in 1907, his early boats were the *Alton*, the *Reliance* built in 1911 and the *Alert*. These boats were engaged in a variety of

The *Messenger*

THE MASCOT OF THE NEUMAN BOAT LINE, SANDUSKY, KELLEYS ISLAND PUT-IN-BAY ROUTE

The *Mascot*

non-scheduled trips for freight, fish, and charter service.

He built the *Messenger* in 1921 and served the Island early and late in the navigation season, when other boats were not running. The *Mascot* joined the *Messenger* in 1925. Two planks were put down from the *Messenger* to the dock, and cars had to be driven onto the boat over the planks, a somewhat precarious and time-consuming manner for loading vehicles.

In 1940, after the *City of Hancock* stopped its service to the islands, Neuman started regular scheduled trips during the entire navigation season with increased frequency during the height of the tourist season. The trip from Sandusky took about an hour and a quarter, and when the boat cleared the Marblehead Lighthouse coming out of Sandusky Bay, depending on the weather, the trip might be an hour's delight, or a stomach churning interminable time.

The boats carried passengers, and everything else to the Island. Harvested grapes had to go to market, and Neuman had grape runs from Kelleys Island and other neighboring islands in the fall of the year. Appliances and furniture could be delivered to the Neuman warehouse on the Sandusky dock, and from there they would make the crossing to Kelleys. Neuman continued to add boats to his line: *Commuter* (1945), *Challenger* (1947), and the flat-topped auto ferries: *Corsair* (1955), *Commuter* (1960), *Kelley Islander* (1969), the *Endeavor* (1987), and the excursion ship *Emerald Empress* (1994). The flat topped ferries had several advantages over the older boats. They had a ramp that went between the dock and the full width of the boat that allowed cars to be easily driven both on and off the boats. Today the flat topped ferries are designed to be docked from either end. Passengers can drive their cars forward onto the boat, stay in straight lines for the passage, and when the destination is reached start their cars and drive off forward again. In the 1950's Neuman purchased property on the southwest corner of Kelleys Island, and in Marblehead, and began more frequent, regularly scheduled trips. This route decreased the time of the boat trip from more than an hour to about twenty minutes. More frequent boat service opened the Island to more tourism, and it also made it easier for service and delivery trucks to come.

The Neuman Boat Line was a family business, with first John P. Neuman, then son Harold Neuman, then his son John Neuman as the principal boat pilots. The term "pilot" was in common usage on Kelleys Island until around the 1950's, when it was gradually replaced by "captain" which is the word used today. John's wife Virginia Neuman was vice-president of the company and instrumental in marketing the firm, along with their son Daniel. Daughter Anne Neuman also worked in the business. Mike Neuman, another one of John and Virginia Neuman's children was a Neuman ferry boat captain for a few years, before continuing his career on larger vessels. Frequently, a passenger was greeted at the Marblehead ticket booth by a member of the Neuman family. John and Virginia Neuman expanded their Kelleys Island dock by adding a building that was partially a warehouse,

The *Shirley Irene* during one of its many daily crossings from Marblehead to Kelleys Island.

office, and gift shop, with a lighthouse tower. It made a welcoming first glimpse of Kelleys Island. At the height of the Neuman Boat Line business, four passenger boats were in operation.

In 1994 the Neuman Boat Line introduced its cruise boat the *Emerald Empress*, that was built and then commissioned as a luxury tourist vessel. Unfortunately, the luxury cruise business waned in the western basin of Lake Erie, and she was eventually sold. The Neuman Boat Line gave service to the Island for 94 years before making its last trip on October 28, 2001. The boats and docks were purchased by the already operating Kelleys Island Ferry Boat Lines. The end of one family's navigation history with Kelleys Island was the beginning of another's service to the Island.

Kelleys Island Ferry Boat Lines

In February, 1991 James Palladino entered the ferry business with his Kelleys Island Ferry Boat Lines. He was the owner of the operating quarry, having previously purchased Kellstone, and now he was ready to start a ferry service from Marblehead to Kelleys Island both for his quarry needs and for passenger service. He designed the first boat in his fleet and had it custom built. It was the biggest flat-topped ferry that had ever serviced Kelleys Island. The boat was named the *Shirley Irene*, after Mr. Palladino's mother. He purchased a second ferry and named her *Kayla Marie*, after a grand-daughter. When he purchased the Neuman boats, he re-painted them in his company colors of blue and orange, and re-named them after grand-daughters: *Carlee Emily*, *Juliet Alicia*, and *Joelle Ann Marie*. His first boat sailed from docks in Sandusky, but he immediately bought property for a dock in Marblehead and on July 4th, 1991, he began regular scheduled ferry service between his Marblehead dock to his dock on Kelleys Island, Seaway Marina, located within walking distance of the downtown commercial area. Mr. Palladino operates his ferry service almost year-round. Generally the boats continue to make trips through December, or until the lake freezes too much to continue. He begins service as early as the weather allows every late winter. During the summer months, the ferries run every half hour from Marblehead and Kelleys Island for many hours every day, sometimes until late in the evening.

Seaway Marina is located on the site of Kelley's Pond, originally owned by the Kelley family. Before development as a marina the road went between the pond and the lake, on a narrow piece of land. A marina had been talked about in that location for many years. When Walter Brown was Mayor of Kelleys Island in 1939, he proposed that the village purchase the property to develop into a public marina. The financing would be done through the selling of revenue bonds to raise $6,000, but when put to the vote the voters turned down the project. The marina idea then waited until 1958 when three investors from Akron bought the property from the then owner Dr. Hummel and started dredging. The plan was for home sites, dockage, and a restaurant, all of which was accomplished, but at a rather low level of commerce.

While the dredging was being done, a record of natural and geologic history was exposed for the first time. About ten feet below the pond level the workers encountered the remains of a dense woods of poplar, cottonwood, beech, and ash. Ohio Wesleyan University identified the species and the University of Michigan radio-carbon dated the material to about 3,270 years ago (with a 200 year variance). During that era, the lake level was much lower than today, and the wooded area extended into what today is covered by lake water. Also found were bones of moose, elk, and deer. The animals would have walked across what had been a big marsh between current day Marblehead and the south shore of Kelleys Island.

In November, 1981 James Palladino saw the potential and purchased the property. He began to expand and develop it into a first class marina, making improvements constantly. He enlarged it

and designed dock spaces on the marina's southeast corner. Some improvements were obvious such as pavement in parking lots and walkways, and others were infrastructure needs such as replacing old waterlines and gasoline storage tanks. Today Seaway Marina, with one hundred permanent slips, and additional floaters, is one of the largest marinas available to summer pleasure boaters. It has a new building that houses a restaurant and shop for boaters' supplies. Picnic table pavilions were built on the grounds around the docks, and golf carts can be rented on the premises.

Architectural Treasures

Kelley Mansion

The Kelley Mansion, as it is now called, stands at the corner of Addison Street and East Lakeshore Drive. It is an imposing two story Italianate Revival home with a widow's walk at the top of the structure. With its native limestone and intricate wood details, it is a beautiful example of Civil War era architecture. It was built by Addison Kelley as his permanent home. J.B Merrick of Sandusky was the architect, the same architect was used for the Kelley Hall (town hall). It was under construction from 1862 to 1867. It was difficult to complete until the Civil War was over. The home has huge elongated win-

Detail of Kelley Mansion

Addison Kelley in front of his home on East Lakeshore Drive

dows that offer a spectacular view of the Marblehead peninsula; the interior has carved woods including cherry, butternut, chestnut, and black walnut; and stained and etched glass. The oak spiral staircase inside the home is a replica of a circular stairway in London, England, built by an English "artificer" who happened to be visiting his brother in New York City at the close of the Civil War. Mr. Kelley hired him to duplicate the stairway in his new Kelleys Island home. In Santa Fe, New Mexico, there is a similar stairway in a chapel. The story told there is that an itinerant carpenter, a foreigner, was passing through when the nuns needed a stairway. He built them an unsupported wooden circular stairway, a little later than that of the Kelley Mansion. It is not hard to imagine that it may be the same woodworker, as he traveled west to see the United States.

The Kelley Mansion has passed through successive owners, some respectful of its mid-nineteenth century essence and others not. In 1928 the home passed from Kelley hands to the Cleveland Sportsman's Club, and was sold again in 1933 to the Dominican Sisters of Adrian, Michigan. It was first used as a retirement home for nuns and later as a summer camp for girls, from 1945 until 1972. About 100 girls, aged 6 to 16, attended during the summer and the camp offered more than 30 subjects taught by counselors and teachers. At this time the Sisters added some of the outbuildings to the grounds.

The Lemley family purchased the house in 1972 with the intent of making it a commercial venture as a hotel and tourist attraction. With that focus, the interior was re-decorated in a more flamboyant manner, including red-flocked wallpaper and glitter in textured plaster. This was the beginning of a long decline to the structure. Eventually parts began falling off the building and lack of maintenance was apparent from the street. Many Island residents were saddened and feared that the house had reached a point beyond repair.

After trying for several years, Edward and Frances Kuchar were able to purchase the Kelley mansion in July, 2003. Mr. Kuchar is a private businessman who owns other properties and homes on Kelleys Island, and has a life-long interest and connection with the Island. He has the historic interest to restore the house to its original grandeur. At this moment Mr. Kuchar is in the middle of the restoration project, which he expects to take several years.

Around their house, the Kelley family had planted many species of trees, including a Dawn Redwood. However, by the time that the Kuchars purchased the property, many of the trees were infested with insects and had been neglected too long to save. Decades of overgrowth also had to be removed from back areas of the property.

Windows have been replaced, the cupola has a new copper roof, new support brackets were made for the cupola and house overhangs, overhangs and soffits have been re-built, rain gutters have been replaced, the interior plaster walls have been sanded to remove the non-historic textured surface, columns were put in the basement to support the first floor beams and the center brick stanchions were replaced under the floor. Chimneys were re-mortared, and new roofs installed, front and side porches re-built, and exterior support columns replaced-all to restore the mansion to its early greatness and to preserve the house for the future. The project encompasses more than just restoration; many times the Kuchars chose to use contemporary materials to ensure longevity over traditional materials. They also decided to better some items, such as installing gutters of copper instead of the original material. There is still much interior work to be done, both structural and decorative. Mr. Kuchar also has had the furniture refinished in readiness to be returned to the house in the future.

Edward Kuchar has an intimate connection with Kelleys Island and boyhood memories of the Kelley Mansion. Both his grandmother, Mrs. Siloy, and his mother Jeannette Siloy Kuchar, worked as cooks for summer camps on the Island. Mrs. Siloy worked summers for the "Villa" Catholic Camp on the north side. In 1956 Jeannette Kuchar worked for the Dominican Sisters at their Kelley Mansion summer camp. Jeannette Kuchar continued to live on Kelleys year-round until her death. Three Kuchar brothers had homes on Kelleys Island and one, Anthony Kuchar was elected Mayor.

Otto Brown's Queen Anne style home is still an architectural jewel on Division Street.

The Otto Brown House

The Otto Brown House stands in the area known as Sweet Valley, on the west side of Division Street across from and just north of the cemetery. The land was said to be some of the best and deepest on Kelleys Island. The area is positioned on the edge of an ancient shoreline. At one time there were two islands, next to each other, and over many thousands of years the space between the islands filled in and became the area known as Sweet Valley. Brown grew grapes and was a vintner, producing both wine and brandy. The Otto Brown house was built by Charles Dodge in 1892, a relative of Brown. It is the best example of Queen Anne style architecture on the Island. The house has not suffered any major changes, additions or alterations, on the exterior or interior since its construction.

Otto Brown was a major figure in the Kelleys Island wine industry. He was the foreman for a number of years with the Kelley's Island Wine Company, and in 1879 he began his own winery. In 1887 Brown began the Sweet Valley Wine Company, with other Islanders. It was named after the location, next to his home, and became the second largest winery on Kelleys Island. There he served as general manager for a number of years before starting the Union Wine Company around the turn of the century. The last wine company to use the building was also the last of the "winery era", the Monarch Winery, which closed in the 1950's.

Himmelein House, East Lakeshore Drive

The Himmelein House

The Himmelein House is located on the south shore of the Island, on East Lakeshore Drive between Division Street and Addison Road. It is undoubtedly the first house noticed by visitors as they approach the Island on a ferry. This Victorian hotel is by far the largest wooden structure on the Island. It stands three stories high, a height dwarfed by its width facing the street. It was built around 1859 by Johann and Johanna Himmelein as a three room home on four acres purchased from Alfred S. Kelley by land contract. The 1860 census shows the family living in the house. The deed to the property was made in 1864. Around 1861, the Himmeleins had boarders, and in the 1870 census Johann Himmelein was listed as a hotel keeper.

In 1875 two wings were added followed in 1882 by the third floor and a central turret. After these additions, the hotel could house one hundred guests. After Johann Himmelein's death, Johanna's sons, Charles, John and Richard, continued to help their mother and made many improvements to the property with additional buildings, including a summer kitchen, livery stable, and a water tower with a pump for running water. The hotel advertised a bathing beach, bath house and a hotel dining room that could serve 125 guests. A bowling alley with a billiard room was erected to the east of the hotel in 1886. This building was converted to a summer cottage after the Himmelein hotel ceased operation in 1915, and is still used as such today. By 1920, shares of the holdings were divided among the heirs and the building was converted into a summer residence for part of the family, which it remains.

The William Dean Kelley House

This Gothic Revival home sits on the south shore, on West Lakeshore Drive, just a few doors west of the downtown business district. It is situated on the east bank of the bed of the once Tiber River and was the third of four houses in a row that were built and occupied by Kelley descendants. It is a spectacular example of Carpenter Gothic architecture. Built in 1861 on land purchased from George Kelley, it features dominant scroll cut balustrades and friezes, with a gothic arched window on the second floor facing front. William Dean Kelley and his second wife Marcella were living on their farm at the north end of Division Street prior to constructing this house on the south shore. The next two generations of William Kelleys used the house as a summer home. While still owned by a Kelley descendant, the house suffered a fire in the kitchen area towards the rear. The burned section was re-built and the entire house was modernized by the Lovins family after their purchase of the property near the end of the twentieth century.

Former William Dean Kelley house, on West Lakeshore Drive

National Register of Historic Places

In 1988, Kelleys Island was placed on the National Register of Historic Places. This came about after a group, headed by Kevin and Betty Pape, became interested in compiling an extensive inventory of older buildings that still remained standing and that were at least 50 years old. It was a registry not only of each building's history, but woven throughout the descriptions is something of the social history of the Island. The Ohio Historical Society reviewed the document and commented that the petition was "Ohio's...first comprehensive historic district encompassing prehistoric and historic archeology, as well as history/architectural resources and significance."

Many elements of architectural styles that were popular in their day, like Victorian, Queen Anne, and Greek Revival, were intermixed in Kelleys Island buildings, exhibiting not only personal and local choices, but also availability of raw materials. Two unique Tudor-style houses stand side by side on the east side of Division Street. Unlike the more prevalent quarried limestone used for foundations and buildings, they were built out of round glacial erratics by local stone mason Godfried Schock. Schock used local materials and was responsible for many stone fireplaces and chimneys in Kelleys Island homes. He came from Germany as a young man to an aunt's house, bringing his craft with him. He worked, married, and lived the rest of his life on Kelleys Island.

Old Stone Church - Originally the German Reformed Church, it was built in 1867 from limestone quarried on the site, on Division St. It is now used by the Kelleys Island Historical Association.

Kelleys Island Historical Association and the Old Stone Church

The Kelleys Island Historical Association seeks to preserve, interpret, and promote the Island's history. It has a museum on Division Street in a stone building that was once the German Reformed Church, now affectionately called the Old Stone Church. The congregation was organized in 1865 and the church was built two years later from stone quarried on the property. Regular services were held in German until the early 1900's when the congregation became too small to support the church. The church building is made of native limestone and has its original windows, interior and bell tower. In 1977, the church and grounds were deeded to the United Church of Christ to try to save the property. No services were held there.

In 1981 the Kelleys Island Historical Association leased the church building to be used as a museum and obtained ownership in 1985. It began immediately to restore and preserve the property. Next to the church building is the new home of the Historical Association. It is a large contemporary structure on the site of the livery stable that belonged to the original church. The stable was a long narrow wooden structure, open to the north, or church side, with a shed roof. The new building was designed to be an echo of that structure. In keeping with local architecture, the stone in the wall facing the street was quarried on Kelleys Island, cut, and placed by a stone mason in 2005. Lafarge, the current quarry operator allowed the stone mason to choose the stone in its quarry and then donated it to the museum. The new museum building will house Kelleys Island memorabilia and a gift shop.

Fishing

Commercial fishing was once an important Island industry. At first fishing was done only in Sandusky Bay with seine nets, but in 1852 there was a revolution in fishing when pound nets were introduced. After the use of pound nets, white fish formed about two thirds of the catch, followed by herring. White fish had a season in the fall and again in the spring and rarely came into Sandusky Bay, but the pound nets set outside the Bay caught them. Pound net fishing continued into the twentieth century. In 1908 there were sixteen locations mostly around the south and east shores of Kelleys Island for pound nets. During the summer months, the net was made and mended by the fishermen with needle and twine, then dipped in hot tar and spread out to dry on the beach or in a pasture. The net was composed of an entrance, called the "leader" that guided the fish into a deeper larger bag or bowl-like area, which held the fish until the nets were lifted. The leader could be twenty feet wide and from a quarter to a half mile long. The trap portion was from twenty to thirty feet square. Since the fish could swim freely inside the larger area of the trap net, the nets did not have to be lifted every day. The nets were secured in place by thirty to forty foot long poles, sharpened at one end, that were pounded into the lake bottom at straight lines radiating outward from the shoreline, by a pile driver on a scow. The "pound" required constant monitoring. Heavy seas and winds could wreck it completely.

By the 1920's the stakes of the pound nets were being replaced by an anchor at each end and floats along the net's edge to hold it up. This method was called trap net fishing. These nets could be easily moved around in the lake to place them ahead of schools of fish. Norman Hills in *A History of Kelley's Island, Ohio*, recounts that there was a market for white fish, muskellunge, black bass, and large pike. Sturgeon, perch, mullet, and saugers had less value and herring and sheepshead were turned into fertilizer in factories in Sandusky. While many families fished to augment their income, some families were dedicated to fishing. Some of the early commercial fishermen's names are J.E. Woodford, Andrew Cameron, Hugh Cattanach, Jared Titus, and later were John and

Herman Koster built his dock in 1889. It was used for shipping wine barrels initially. Later it was used by Lay Bros. for their fishing boats.

Homer Woodford, John Reinheimer, Peter and John Ditchie, Sylvester Dwelle, and Fred Dischinger. The Sylvester Dwelle family, on the east end of the Island, fished in flat bottomed boats nearer to shore while J.E. Woodford fished in deeper waters farther from the Island shoreline. In 1880, two brothers, Peter and John Ditchie, came to the Island to fish commercially. They started the Sandusky Fish Company. Their home and their twine shanty (1893) were located on the south shore on what is known as Sunrise Point. The twine shanty was used to store fishing equipment, especially the nets. The area was still used for mending nets as late as the 1950's. The twine shanty has since been converted into Sunrise Point Motel and the Ditchie house is now Annalee's Lakeshore Cottage.

After Peter Ditchie married Julie Monaghan and moved to Pelee Island in Canada, John continued in

Trap net fishermen pulling in their net. They worked from a boat pulled behind a larger boat. The fish could stay alive three to five days in a trap net, so the fishermen are lifting and dumping live fish into the boat. The south shore of Kelleys Island is in the background.

the fishing industry and expanded his business to Koster's Dock. This unusual dock building lies at the foot of Addison Road and West Lakeshore Drive and is now operated as a private club and marina, called Unique Marker Yacht Club. Herman Koster built the dock and storage building in 1883 to handle the shipping needs of his winery. The dock was subsequently used by the Sweet Valley, Monarch, and Meiers Wine companies for shipping. The projecting wood canopy shelters the original entrance to the shipping house and supported block and tackle equipment that was used to lift wine barrels from the dock to the boats. In 1907 Kelleys Island Lime & Transport purchased the dock and laid a cable for the first private telephone system on the Island, used to connect its Island office with its mainland office. In the 1920's and 1930's Lay Brothers Fish Company, based on the mainland, tied some of its boats at Koster's Dock and used the Ditchie twine shanty.

About the same time that trap nets and gill nets came into use, engines were added to the commercial fishing boats. A net winder that was once used to

The *Pal* was built by Art Beatty on Kelleys Island as a gill netting boat for Mike Riedy. A gill netting boat had higher sides on it than a boat that was built for trap net fishing. This was a common fishing boat shape around Kelleys Island.

pull nets from the loaded boats still remains on Koster's dock (now the Unique Marker Yacht Club). Gill nets were less expensive to purchase than the trap nets, but they had to be lifted every day. They are set in deeper waters with power boats. Schools of fish are caught in the nets and then the nets must be lifted before the fish die. The fishermen pulled up the gill net, emptied the fish, and then reset the net ahead of the school of fish. Mike Riedy was one of the last commercial gill net fishermen. Today, gill netting is no longer legal in the State of Ohio. Riedy's dock was on

the south shore, at the base of Division Street and West Lakeshore Drive. His boat house and marine garage were sold after his death to Burt Miller. After Miller, the building was sold again several times and is now converted into a gift shop, known as Kelleys Cove, operated by Don and Sandy Alexander.

Independent Island fishermen would sell their catch to the Lay Brothers Company. Between 1930 and 1960, the north bay was also used as a base for commercial fishing boats. The Lay Brothers made an arrangement with KIL&T Company to use the dock area and parts of the then inactive north quarry. Traces of tar can still be seen on some of the rocks in that area, where freshly tarred nets had been laid out to dry. Remnants of piles of metal net floats, looking like elongated tin cans, are also found in parts of the State Park on the north side of the Island. During the winter months, after ice of sufficient thickness formed in the lake, the fishermen cut ice and stored it in an ice house on the north bay. The foundation of the ice house is still visible, now part of the State Park complex. The ice was sold and delivered to the Islanders during the summer months for their home ice boxes, the precursors of today's refrigerator.

In 1956 the Kelleys Island Fish Producers Co-op purchased Koster's Dock to use as a base for some of the last commercial fishing by Kelley Islanders. The industry would not last. Low prices and major pollution problems in Lake Erie created by the steel and other industries both in the United States and Canada, caused the fish to dwindle and led to a state ban on commercial fishing. This finally caused a major exodus of families from the Island. Younger members of families moved off the Island and had to find work that they were able to do as ex-fishermen. Many times they moved to city areas to work in factories.

Sport Fishing

By the late 1970's the lake pollution was cleaned up and sport fishing came into importance, an echo of the 1870's when tourists came for spring and fall fish runs. The Island fishing grounds are close to deeper cold waters that are the preference for many of the larger game fish. Sportsman's clubs began to invest in Island property. The Cleveland Sportsman's Club purchased the Kelley Mansion in the late 1920's, but closed during the Depression. On the west side, the Kelleys Island Sportsman's Club was established in 1939, (now known as the West End Club near Carpenter's Point). They also stocked the Island with young pheasants for many years, for hunting.

Today sport fishing is bigger and better than ever and attracts fisherman from early spring to late fall. Yellow perch are a desirable sport fish and can be caught year-round near shore areas: from the shoreline, piers, and boats. The best season is from August through October. The western basin of Lake Erie is referred to as "the Walleye capital of the world" and they are most plentiful from June through August around the Island areas and western Lake Erie reefs. Schools of white bass are usually encountered in May and June. Smallmouth bass have two main seasons, May and June and again in August through October. Freshwater drum, also known as sheepshead and channel catfish, also deliver good sport fishing in June and July. Many local businesses like Kelleys Cove, Uncl' Dik's, Crafts, and Seaway Marina supply bait, tackle, dockage, and Ohio licenses to sport fishermen.

Albert "Scoop" McKillips, Albert Kugler and Sylvester "Sonnee" Dwelle hold up an 180 pound sturgeon that they caught near Kelleys Island on April 20, 1935. It was the largest sturgeon caught in the Great Lakes.

Ice Fishing

Ice shanties on the north bay.

Ice Fishing is a traditional winter past time. Islanders ice fished for food and profit for generations, hauling their shanties onto the ice wherever they thought the fishing would be good. A hole is made in the ice inside the shanty and a stool or chair is brought in, along with a stove so that the angler can be comfortable while he waits for a bite. Usually yellow perch and walleye are most often the fish of choice, although sometimes white bass are also found. The ice has to be at least six inches thick to be safe for fishing and it is always a difficult decision about when to end the season by pulling the shanty to shore. When the weather starts to warm, the ice can move very quickly creating a dangerous situation. Over the years there have been many near mishaps of ice fishermen stranded on ice flows, as well as lost vehicles and lost ice shanties.

Rescue on the Lake

It might have been different; six souls lost, instead of three souls saved.

The Island fishermen always dreaded northeast gales. On Kelleys Island the New England expression "nor'easter" is used as well as "northeaster." Lake Erie being the shallowest of the Great Lakes, the gales can come up quickly and usually last for three days, the third day being a "dead roll", with the waves continuing to roll into the Island although the wind had already stopped. Since Kelleys Island is the farthest east of the Lake Erie island group, once the wind starts to blow from Buffalo, there is nothing to break up the momentum of the lake. The wind builds and pushes mountains of water into the east end of the Island. The lake has reached record heights during northeast storms, causing flooding at its shoreline, destruction, erosion, and loss of lives. It can be especially treacherous even for the experienced boat pilot, whether a commercial sea captain or a pleasure boater. Weather has its own long rhythms and the years between 1857 and 1862 saw some of the greatest storms of the nineteenth century. In August of 1861 the main dock at Kelleys Island was destroyed by such a gale storm.

1902 was another year of unusually violent northeasters. On the 28th of June, 1902 a powerful storm occurred. Islanders had gone down to the shore at the east end of the Island to watch the huge waves crash in one after the other. The steamer George Dunbar had left Cleveland, Ohio bound for Alpena, Michigan, with a crew of ten people. During the night a gale force storm had come up, and the George Dunbar began to struggle through it. Somewhere east of Kelleys Island it foundered and sank. Five of the crewmen took a life raft, but they couldn't stay afloat in the raging sea and were drowned. Captain Little, his wife, his grown daughter, and two other crewmen left the ship in a yawl boat, but that soon capsized also, and the crewmen were lost. Captain Little and his family had life preservers and managed to stay afloat. They were in the raging water for many hours before they passed the east end of Kelleys Island. Amongst the Kelley Islanders watching from the shore were neighbors that lived on the east end, Fred Dischinger (about 56 yrs. old), his son Fred, Jr. (about 21 yrs. old), and Island Mayor James Hamilton (about 48 yrs. old). Fred Dischinger Sr. was known as an experienced fisherman. The pounding roar of the surf made it difficult to tell if they heard a person cry out or something else. Then they saw something out in the surf, above the breakers, but couldn't be sure if it was birds, parts of trees, or a person. They decided that the movement was a head bobbing up and down. Most of the Islanders watching the terrible scene thought that it was impossible to attempt a rescue. But, the three men found a flat bottomed skiff which they dragged to the water. They launched the boat and headed into the roaring sea. Two men rowed while one man constantly bailed until they reached the shipwrecked family. The three men determined right away that there was no way to get the three people into the little skiff, so they threw a rope to Captain Little who managed to fasten it to his life preserver and then to his wife and daughter. The two Dischingers and Hamilton then rowed back to the shoreline where other Islanders could help pull the three castaways on to the shore. The shipwrecked people had been in the water so

A milk weed pod dangles from its stem in the fall of the year. Milk weed was once plentiful on the Island. Monarch butterflies, which need milk weed in the caterpillar stage, stop by in the thousands on their way to Mexico.

long that they were completely blue. At least one was unconscious and the other two almost. None would have lived much longer if they had not been rescued. Captain Little and his family stayed with an Island family for a few weeks while they recuperated from their ordeal.

The deed of the three Island men was deemed so heroic that it was brought to the attention of the U.S. Congress. Each man, Fred Dischinger Sr, Fred Dischinger Jr, and James Hamilton, received a gold medal with his name inscribed on it, awarded by an Act of Congress "For heroic daring in saving life, June 29, 1902."

The Seasons

The seasons on Kelleys Island align with the northern part of the United States except that being situated in Lake Erie modifies them slightly. Spring arrives later, sometimes by several weeks, than on the mainland. The lake that cooled down all winter now cools the air as it crosses over it before reaching the Island. Daffodils and Hyacinths start blooming later than in nearby Sandusky, but keep blooming much longer.

The other season that has a marked difference is the fall of the year. When the leaves are off the trees

Pockets of maple trees form vibrant colors. Some are sugar maples which locals tap for syrup in the spring.

in other parts of northern Ohio, they are just beginning to turn color on Kelleys Island. The Island has pockets of Sugar Maples in reds and yellows. They make a dramatic contrast with the blue berried Red Cedar trees, once prized as fire wood for steam boat boilers. The autumn is much longer than on the mainland. The lake has been heating all summer, and it cools down slowly. As the winds cross the lake, they warm up and thus give the Island a slow mellow time to get ready for the winter storms.

The bleakest and slowest time of the year is winter. The Island can sustain some high winds during the winter and early spring months. While traditionally not known as the snow belt, some winters can produce periods of deep snow. Once the lake freezes, travel to and from the Island can only be done during daylight flying weather.

Some of the most spectacular scenery is on the frozen lake. As the weather changes, warm spells followed by cold spells, and warm days followed by cold nights, in the winter and early spring, the lake ice begins to move and to shove up onto the shore. Sometimes it forms high piles of broken ice, sometimes crystal clear panes, ten or more feet across, stand up perpendicular like windows, and some years

there are piles of ice cube-sized and shaped ice, which was once perfect for making ice cream in a hand turned ice cream maker. Every year is a different panorama.

The ice can also make eerie cracking noises when it begins to break up. In the spring of the year, come the ice cakes, separate chunks of ice that float in the water, before completely melting away.

Spring brings wildflowers. Before the deer arrived, the Island was covered with wildflowers. Unfortunately through deer grazing and human development, many of the flowers are no longer present. The change from farm land to brush has also made some wildflowers decline. Up to the mid twentieth century the pastures were filled with buttercups, daisies, Queen Anne's lace, and blue cornflowers.

Cold winter winds blow across the ice on the southwest shore.

Dottie Simonds retired to Kelleys Island. Here she is standing in front of a pile of ice that shoved onto the shoreline. The alternating freezing and thawing of the lake ice, usually in the early spring, cuts the ice into every size, from ice cubes to huge vertical sheets that look like panes of window glass.

Summer in the State Park on the trail to North Pond off Ward Road.

Cedar trees at the corner of Woodford and Monagan roads. Cedar trees covered Kelleys Island in the 1800's and were forested in large numbers to fuel steam boats.

Turtles sunning on Monagan Road

Titus Road, known as Lovers' Lane, passes through the north woods.

59

In spring, May Apples form dense carpets of leafy green in the woods on the north side.

Above: Trillium was once plentiful in the north woods, both white and red. Now they are a rare sight. The deer population has decimated many of the traditional wildflowers.

May Apples

Right: Dutchman's Britches are a wild relative of the Bleeding Heart family of plants. They are one of the spring treasures on Kelleys Island, where they still grow in abundance in a few areas.

Today the buttercups have gone, but the others can still be seen along the roadsides during the mid to late summer months. Early spring brings Dutchman's britches, trillium, spring beauties, adder's tongues, jack-in-the pulpits, and May apples, though in less profusion than in earlier years. Most of these are seen along roadsides or along the State Park trails.

The Lakeside daisy, a rare plant, was brought to Kelleys Island from the nearby mainland Lakeside-Marblehead. Grown on limestone alvars, they were brought to Kelleys Island to colonize. The experiment worked well, and today there are fields of Lakeside daisies in the State Park on the north side of the Island. The most endangered wildflowers are the trillium that are rarely found today. Summer brings out wild roses and purple roadside asters, and finally in autumn, the wild bittersweet finishes the season.

The Island is an isolated area and has both native animals and more recent arrivals. It is a stopover for migrating birds and butterflies. When the Island was less developed, there were areas of milkweed which attracted Monarch butterflies. Migrating birds stop on their way to summer and winter homes. Today the American bald eagle has returned to Kelleys Island. Off and on through time, bald eagles have nested on the Island. The earliest record, oral, of bald eagle nests pre-dates 1838, when Sylvestor Dwelle came to the Island and noted them. Kurt Boker records twelve sites of bald eagle nests in his essay "The When and Where of Bald Eagle Nests on Kelleys Island." All but one of the nests was built in the eastern half of the Island, probably to avoid the noise and activity from quarrying operations. In 2005, a pair of bald eagles built a nest on the north side of the Island, in the State Park area. During the winter a young eagle has sometimes been seen on the ice or flying.

At one time pheasants were on the Island, as long as their numbers were re-stocked every year by a private hunting club (the Kelleys Island Sportsman's Club), and they had farm land. When farming ceased, pheasants had less food and cover for over wintering. This happened at the same time that raccoons came to the Island and they ate the pheasants' eggs. The combination has proved deadly. Even though groups of people have tried to re-establish pheasants from time to time, nothing has worked on a permanent basis.

The Island is an isolated eco-system. Plants and animals could only come to the Island by natural means, flying or swimming, before human habitation. The most changes in flora and fauna have occurred after the increase in movement of residents between the mainland and the Island and through tourism. The raccoons established themselves after someone released raccoons they had brought from the mainland. Deer also are rumored to have been brought from the mainland in the 1960's. The Island has a lot of thistles growing today since people have fed birds in the winter with untreated thistle seed. The Japanese beetle came to the Island on plants from gardens off-Island, around the 1950's, and the brown recluse spider came later with campers.

In recent years, coyotes have also established themselves on the Island and there have been several dens discovered in the quarry areas. In 2006 the greatest threat came from the emerald ash borer insect which the U.S. Dept. of Agriculture had found in all of Erie County except Kelleys Island. Since the emerald ash borer is a poor flyer and can only fly about a half mile annually, the threat of contamination comes through infected firewood transported by tourists for campfires. Kelleys Island has over fifty percent ash trees, so devastation by the insect would change the look of the Island once again. In 2007, the insect was found on the Island.

Waterfowl are a common sight: mallard ducks, Canadian geese, merganzers, cormorants, bufflehead ducks, and seagulls. Muskrats, called locally "marsh squirrel", were once plentiful on the Island and in the fall, people made muskrat stew, a rather

Lakeside daisy

Field of Lakeside daisies in the State Park alvar area

gamey tasting concoction. There are more rabbits some years than others, depending on the number of predators around. Fox seem to come and go. Both they and the coyotes have come over in the winter on the ice.

This brings us to another traditional part of the Island's critters—snakes. Snakes have always been prevalent on Kelleys Island and they are mentioned in some of the oldest accounts of the Island. The last rattlesnake seen on Kelleys Island was in 1914, off Titus Road, but today there are no poisonous snakes. The Island has an abundance of water snakes, fox snakes, blue racers and common garter snakes. The fox snakes are associated with the quarry areas and the water snakes with the shoreline. On warm, sunny days, you may encounter a snake sunbathing on a dock or on the limestone rocks along the shore or in the quarries. Nerodia sipedon insularum, the Lake Erie water snake, is grey in color, with no distinctive pattern of markings. When the glaciers melted about 4,000 years ago, forming the Great Lakes, some of the populations of the northern water snake were stranded on the Lake Erie islands. Through subsequent genera-

tions, they began to evolve, to help camouflage themselves in their new environment, so that today they are distinctive from the mainland dwelling northern water snake. They have always been plentiful on Kelleys Island, but have been eradicated from other neighboring islands. In 1999, they won a spot on the Federal Endangered Species list. In the spring, when mating, the water snakes can form large balls of writhing snakes rolling along grassy shorelines.

Island Artists

The natural beauty of Kelleys Island is an attraction for visual artists, both hobbyists and professionals. Kelleys Island is a rich mix of nature and domestication. Sunrises and sunsets over the lake are dramatic and colorful in any season. The diversity of plant life and terrain in an area small enough to walk through and around is a constant enticement for inspiration. All of the artists included in this chapter have had some relationship with Kelleys Island.

Henry Frank Dischinger
1841 - 1917

Henry Dischinger, was an immigrant from Baden, Germany, at a time when many Germans came to the area of Port Clinton, Sandusky, and the Lake Erie islands. Soon after arriving in the United States at age 14, he apprenticed to a buggy works in Elmore, Ohio. Eventually he mastered gold striping and leafing and the embellishment of fine carriages. In the 1860 census he is listed in the household of a master painter in Tiffin, Ohio. During that time period, much of the wood used in house interiors was soft wood, and it was the custom for the well-to-do to have the wood trim and doors painted to look like more expensive hard wood, or floors to look like marble or carpeting. Dischinger worked as a sign painter and interior house painter (decorator) which included the application of faux finishes, like wood graining and marbling. By nature this is an itinerant occupation, the craftsman moving from house to house and community to community, where ever his work might take him.

Henry's brother Fred lived with his family on Kelleys Island and when Henry visited them, he also painted. There exists at least one faux finished door signed by Henry Dischinger in a house on the south

Oil paintings by Henry Dischinger

could be characterized as American Primitives and the best as an extension of the Hudson River School. The subject matter for his oil paintings was generally of things in his personal experience, of scenery, especially farms, hunting dogs, and woods with deer. Henry Dischinger's home was first in Port Clinton, while most of his adult life he resided around the Elmore, Ohio area. Some of his larger oil paintings are on view in the Elmore City offices, bank, and library. In 1966 the Dischinger homestead sold all his oil paintings, about 300, that had been in storage, all dated from 1863 onward, with many in original period frames.

Arnold Scheele
1886 - 1973

Arnold Scheele was raised on Kelleys Island in a home on the south shore and graduated from Kelleys Island High School, where he taught for two years before entering Oberlin College. His art talent was obvious early in life and he began art lessons at the age of 11, from a local doctor's wife, Mrs. R. N.

shore. There are also some faux finished floors intact in another home, but it is unclear at this point if they are Dischinger's work. He became well known in the area for his skill as a painter of scenes and in the 1860's and '70's he also painted drop curtains and stage scenery for theatrical productions. In the 1880's Henry Heckman from Elmore, was making wagons and it was recorded that "two fine fruit wagons" were made for Kelleys Island, "in the latest modern style, with Henry Dischinger having done the fine painting work." When the interior decoration was to be done for the new Court House in Port Clinton, Henry Dischinger was hired by the Ottawa County Commissioners as Superintendent on the job, overseeing artists painting murals in the rotunda of the new building. He did much of the stenciling himself along with painting some of the pictures in the smaller rooms.

Henry Dischinger was also a prolific easel painter, and these paintings are what have survived best to present day. Some of his oil paintings are in Kelleys Island homes. He was a great technician and his work was characteristic of the nineteenth century. He obviously had an interest in the styles of his day, not only for his commercial patrons, but also in the fine arts. His paintings reflect that mix; some

Oil paintings by Arnold Scheele

Sheldon. He continued his art training off-island, studying at Wooster University, Johns Hopkins University, the Art Students League in New York, Art Institute of Chicago, American Academy of Art, and the Art Institute of Fontainebleau in France. He studied or traveled every summer with some of the leading artists of his day. Scheele graduated with a B.A. from Oberlin College in 1910 and received his M.A. in 1911 from the same institution. He was Dean of the Commercial Art School in Chicago, Illinois, taught at the University of Illinois and then was head of the Art Department at Michigan State University at Lansing, Michigan. In 1945 he retired after 26 years of teaching at MSU, and then began to split his time between his home in Laguna Beach, California, and his family home on Kelleys Island.

Scheele was an artist with a national reputation for oil paintings of marine scenes, which interest undoubtedly stemmed from his connection with Kelleys Island and Lake Erie. His work was chosen for a traveling show sponsored by the National Artists League of 100 best artists, and he was given a scholarship to study in Europe. Scheele exhibited widely and was interested in having his paintings in people's homes and public institutions. If someone really wanted one of his paintings, he would make it possible for them to have one. He loaned his paintings to both public institutions and private parties. On August 4, 1949, the village of Kelleys Island formally accepted paintings from Arnold Scheele for the town hall. Other paintings were given to Estes School, and also the Catholic and the Protestant Churches on the Island. He did some portraits and still lifes, but his most representative work is of marine scenes. His paintings hang on the walls in many Kelleys Island homes. He never tired of capturing moving water in all its power and mystery.

Joe Corso
1961-

Joe Corso has become a regular figure on Kelleys Island during the end of the twentieth century and can be seen frequently, either on his bicycle scouting a new subject or working at his easel beside a road. Corso prefers camping and foot power to modern conveniences. He is a romantic at heart and his art reflects those choices. Raised in Sandusky, Corso left the area during the second half of the 1980's to study art. He began in photography, but through his first classes in painting and drawing, he realized that he

Oil painting by Joe Corso, whose paintings have been used throughout this book.

liked the total control that a fine artist has in the choices of his work and he discovered his true calling—that of a painter and interpreter of the natural world. He generally works in the open air and focuses on landscapes. Buildings are a secondary interest for him thematically, but he finds architecture interesting and so includes it in his landscapes. Around 1984, he was working on a painting on a street on Kelleys Island, when someone asked him to do a commission for them. Soon many people knew of his talent and wanted paintings of their houses, and he was sought after to paint a remembrance of their special place. Corso has made oil paintings of many of the homes on Kelleys Island, both historic and new, in addition to community events like the one ring tent circus that returns to Kelleys annually.

On Kelleys Island, Corso feels that he can "get away from everything", explore and go places where other people hardly ever go. Commission work involves painting what someone wants, and it is different in style from his foremost interest— landscapes. He prefers the more undeveloped landscapes like those found in the quarry areas. Nature is what attracts and inspires him. He used to go to the deserts of New Mexico and Arizona, and the mountains of Colorado to immerse himself in the "most special places he could think of." He had been to the Island in his youth, and he said that even then he knew there was something special about it. He returns to Kelleys Island because "there are places on Kelleys Island that are as good as it gets." He believes that other people also feel this special quality, even though they may not articulate it. This unspoken thought is what keeps them coming back. Corso captures some of this emotion in his sparse landscapes and "waterscapes". He develops calm and quiet moods in his paintings and tries to pass on optimism. Life in the 21st century can be hectic and demanding, exacting a realism that hardens human beings to the joy of beauty inherent in everyday things. Corso wants to bring some calm into the lives of others through the moods of his painterly work. He characterizes himself as providing a service to people, reminiscent of the itinerant craftsman of past times. He works on trust rather than formal contracts, whether it is an artist patron relationship, or doing odd jobs. There is a strength of faith about Joe Corso, faith in his craft, faith in his art, and faith that it will carry him through to the next day, and to the next painting.

Charles Laylin Herndon
1947-

Charles "Chuck" Herndon has a lifelong connection with Kelleys Island. Raised in Cleveland, when he was young during summers, his family came to his maternal grandmother's home (Laylin family) on the Island. Herndon describes his early years: "I spent a lot of time wandering around on the beach in front of my grandmother's house. I know now, but didn't then, that the island is basically one large chunk of limestone, hard enough to have resisted the erosive power of the glaciers of earlier ice ages. The beach consists of stones, cobbles, pebbles and sand sorted by weight, shape, contour and specific gravity in response to the action of the waves, the ice, and the current. The limestone bedrock has yielded slowly to the waves and to freezing and thawing, as large chunks break off, resulting in drop off shelves, as one enters the water. The chunks that break off are tum-

You Can Tell the Leopard by Her Spots.
Limestone sculpture by Charles Herndon.

bled by wave action, are broken, tumbled and broken again and again. What results is a beach of limestone pieces, rounded but flat."

In college Herndon took a geology class which only served to stimulate his interest more. Herndon's interest in rocks, how they are formed, and how he can sculpt them is still his primary concern. His work derives, in large part, from his experience of the natural features and processes he has observed on the Island. The colored stones found on the beach are classified as glacial erratics. In childhood Herndon touched and examined them, and later he returned to carve them, bringing his childhood "musings into the language of the work."

On describing the crux of his work, Herndon says, "I am concerned with touch and response—investing simple form with significant meaning. The work is allusive, sensual and dense."

"As I walk the beach near my studio and look down at the stones I've crossed time and again over my life . . . As my preparation has improved through education and experience, what the beach offers

Golden Curl by Charles Herndon

65

becomes richer. I see in the stones before me and under me, and in those I take from the beach to carve, the manifestation of history, geology, process and time. At the same time I associate with the shapes, colors, patterns and relationships . . . I see my own history and involvement with art making, my experience of life and the world around me."

Charles Herndon works out of his studios on the east end of Kelleys Island. A sculpture studio was built in 1980 and a painting and photography studio in 2000. As time has gone on and the hazards linked to making sculpture and to teaching in a constantly polluted atmosphere have taken their toll, he has spent an increasing amount of time painting and working on his photographs. Herndon's Gallery on Kelleys Island is open to the public and he has show openings of new work during the summer months.

Charles Herndon has a BFA from the Cleveland Institute of Art, 1971; a BA from Case Western Reserve University in 1969; and an MFA from Syracuse University in 1973.

Claudia Mae Brown
1947-

Brown lives on Kelleys Island property that has been in her family for four generations. She was raised east of Cleveland, Ohio, but since all her relatives lived on Kelleys, her family made frequent visits to the Island throughout each year. In her youth, Brown painted many Kelleys Island landmarks, and although she showed aptitude for painting, in college she majored in ceramics, both stoneware and porcelain. That choice was based in her belief that items of everyday use in people's

A porcelain bowl with inlay by Claudia Brown. A shell was used to make the impressions that were inlaid with a darker clay.

homes are important to the experience of their lives. Surrounding oneself with beautiful, hand made things allows a constant dialogue with the essence of what it is to be human and enriches the human spirit in subtle but powerful ways. After her BFA and working for a year at the Cleveland Museum of Art, she pursued her interest in pottery by entering the Masters program at the University of Minnesota to study with Warren MacKenzie, an internationally recognized functional potter. In the 1980's Brown returned to painting after illness forced her to curtail working with clay. She does easel paintings in watercolor and oil, and uses acrylic for her faux finish and mural work. The mural work returns to the theme of living with art in the home, the artist's presence subtly woven into the fabric of everyday life.

One of the recurring themes in Brown's work, whether in ceramics or painting, is shells. Her first memory of sea shells is collecting them on Sand Beach on Kelleys Island, and picking up snail shells from the bottom of the grooves at Glacial Grooves. The remains and impressions of shells in Kelleys Island limestone also fascinated her, both for their dense sensual volume and for their detail. In the beach shells she appreciated their form, subtle coloring, and the near translucency of some of them. Light skipping on green clear water, translucent shells, fields of white limestone and patterned fossils—these seminal elements were translated into glass (glazes) on stoneware and porcelain, and watercolors.

The use of transparent glazes on clay recalls the shallow waters along the Lake Erie shoreline; thin edges on bowls are memories of shells. Brown's work is subtle in form and color and generally more evocative than dramatic. Shells may be impressed into the side of wet clay for decoration, sometimes inlaid with a contrasting clay color and sometimes a piece of shell becomes a tool in her hands to draw lines or form a pattern. As a further connection with her early Island experiences, Brown has used a shell, cast from an original Island fossil as her maker's mark for years on her clay pieces. This awareness and connection with the natural world Brown attributes to her early connection with Kelleys Island. It constantly enters her life, whether she is residing on the Island or elsewhere. Kelleys Island has always been "home" in the spiritual sense of being the crucible of her early formative experi-

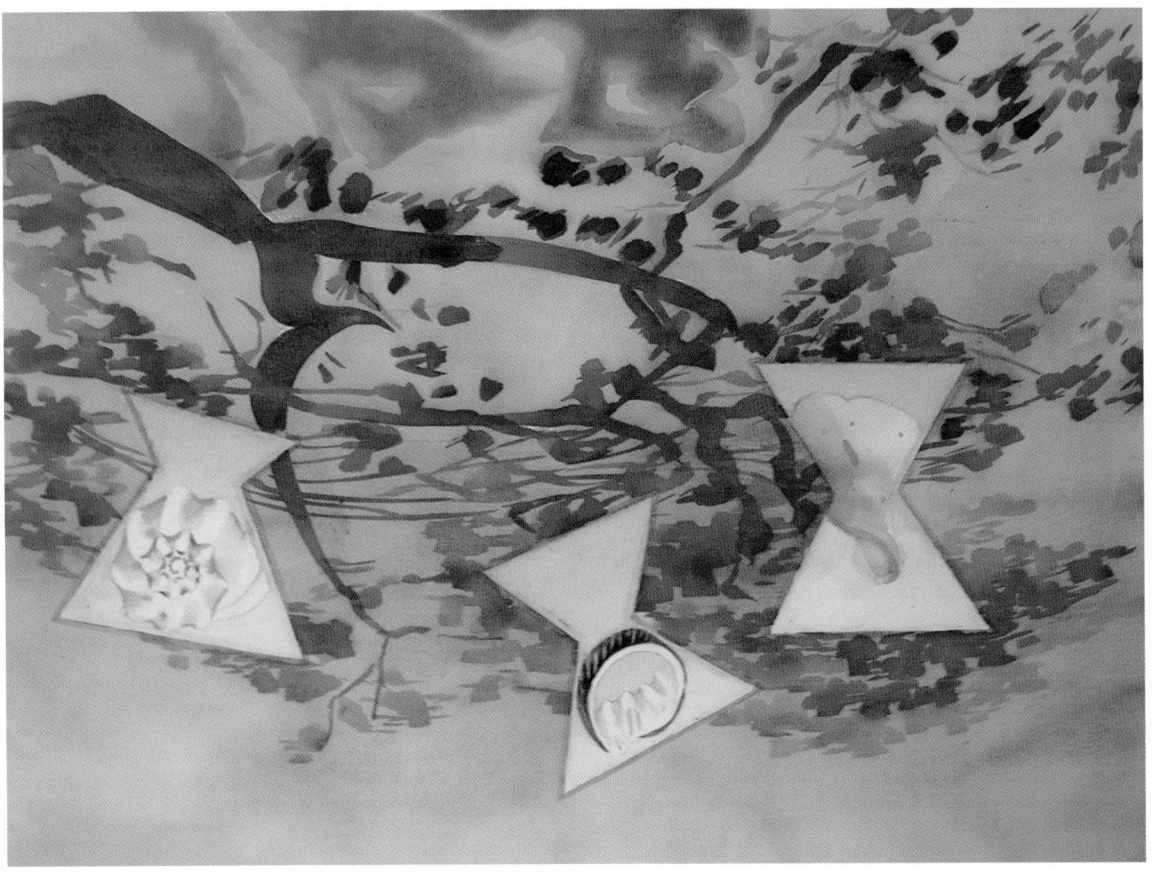

A watercolor by Claudia Brown in her "Portales" series of paintings.

ences. After the zebra mussels came to the lakeshore, most of the shells from Brown's youth disappeared, but occasionally some are still discovered on a walk and a few may still make it into her pocket to become an inspiration.

Brown has a BFA from the Cleveland Institute of Art, in 1970; an MFA from the University of Minnesota, in 1973; and an MS from Fairleigh Dickinson University, in 1982.

The Island Re-Invents Itself

Kelleys Island began as a commercial investment by the Kelley brothers in the nineteenth century. It has gone through many changes in business starting with wood cutting, quarrying, wineries, fishing and farming industries. The Kelley family saw opportunity, and today people still do. Today's commerce is tourism, tourist related activities, and real estate in second homes. It comes alive every spring and quiets down every fall. There are hiking trails in the State Park for the naturalist and walks along streets of historic Victorian houses. On a sunny day along the lakeshore with the lake water sparkling

like diamonds, it is paradise. Streets rim the majority of the Island's circumference, where every view is spectacular: Put-In-Bay to the west, Marblehead and Cedar Point with its roller coasters to the south, open water to the east, and Pelee and Middle Islands in Canada to the north. People walking, biking, roller-blading, and riding in open golf carts all mix with cars on the roads during the summer months. The bar-restaurants are open from May to September, and a few stay open most of the year. The historic names of Kelley, Huntington, Dwelle, Beatty, Monaghan, Elfers, Brown, Riedy, Lange, Martin and more have been replaced by new community leaders. The "summer people" of the 1950's have become the second home property owners of today. Where once the Island was populated by families who rarely left the Island, the majority of the population is now in transit. Every week, they travel to their summer home for the week-end, or swell the population for vacation days and weeks. There is still commercial opportunity for the adept businessman or investor. There is still adventure and a full experience of nature, along isolated trails or narrow Island roads. Commercial fishing has given way to sport fishing.

Boats can be chartered from the Island or mainland, or fishing can be done from the shoreline and docks. A festive atmosphere predominates as vacationers fulfill their expectations in "Ohio's Vacationland."

Many of today's newer residents had experiences with Kelleys Island in their youth, perhaps at some camp, and decided to return for retirement. Some stay just part of each year, going to warmer places during the winter months, and some stay through the whole year, experiencing winter in an Island way. They have brought a vitality to the year-round community, participating in events, joining and volunteering for Island organizations, working in the library, and serving on government boards and committees. The business people included in this chapter are examples of the many people in business who after coming to the Island to develop businesses, have become involved personally in the community.

Since the 1980's, Bob Gruly has been involved in the construction, renovation, and management of many of the Island's commercial establishments. He renovated a downtown restaurant, Marine Grill and Motel, and converted the building into the Porthole Restaurant. It has since been sold and re-named Bag the Moon. Gruly realized that people wanted an easy-to-use, downtown location as a tourist getaway

The Quarry Condominiums and their pond. The pond is part of the oldest quarry.

and the idea of the Quarry Condominiums was born, consisting of nine condo buildings with fifty-four units, a pool, and storage buildings. The condos offered a maintenance-free home, with a lake view at their entrance, quarry lake views to the north and east, a setback from the street for quiet, and easy walking distance to downtown restaurants and activities.

Gruly has also managed the Casino Restaurant and re-built and increased the dockage there. He next moved to the west side, where he worked on the marina that is part of West Bay Inn. This is the only marina that faces Put-In-Bay to the west. He and his wife Pat currently manage the West Bay Inn's Bar and Restaurant.

Around 1992, Kathy and Ken Reddinger purchased the Porthole Restaurant on West Lakeshore Drive and renamed it Bag the Moon Saloon. Kathy trained and joined the Island EMT's. It is a kind of Island phenomenon that the business community extends itself to the main community. Many individuals have become EMT's or have supported the school through special projects.

Patti Johnson is the third generation in her Island business. Her grandmother, Ruth Gibbons, and her parents, Patricia and Jay (William) Johnson, started the first soft serve ice cream stand around the west side of the Island in 1960. Patti has enlarged the building and made a restaurant and brew pub. With an outside patio, the Kelleys Island Brewery has spectacular views of lake sunsets with Catawba Island on the mainland as a backdrop.

Danny Ahner developed property along Division Street, downtown, as Caddy Shack Square. He continued the miniature golf course that fronts the property and added specialty shops towards the rear including the Caddy Shack Restaurant and Bar. Ahner also has real estate properties and developed Sweet Valley Subdivision on Division Street with Albert Fresch.

Gary and Jackie Finger own and operate the Village Pump Bar and Restaurant in a historic building downtown on West Lakeshore Drive. Gary Finger graduated from Estes School on the Island, and Kelleys Island has been his home for many years. Interested in Island history, they have a large collection of Island photographs on permanent view in their restaurant. They also own a historic home on East Lakeshore Drive, once the Moysey Hotel with the original barn behind. As animal lovers they have cats and dogs, horses, and alpacas. The Finger family purchased a building on Woodford Road that was once a twine shanty for commercial fishermen, which they converted from a storage building to a horse barn. They also subdivided property off Woodford Road as Vineyard Estates Subdivision. They are very active members of the Chamber of Commerce. Gary Finger trained as an E.M.T. and served the Island for several years as part of the emergency medical squad. He has also had several terms on the Village Council.

James Palladino is an exceptional entrepreneur and has had many interests since his arrival on Kelleys Island. In business enterprises, he parallels the Kelley family's history of growth and expansion. He was first introduced to Kelleys Island through friends that were boaters, in the 1970's. He then purchased his own boat and began to frequent the Island. James Palladino has worked hard to develop his businesses. His first business on Kelleys was Seaway Marina. Under Mr. Palladino the marina was updated and expanded, and today Seaway Marina is a large, protected, modern marina on the southeast shore, with a cafe restaurant and a store catering to boaters. His second business on the Island was the quarry on the west side, which he ran for a number of years as Kellstone, Inc. He also owns West Bay Inn, bar and restaurant, near the quarry operation. His most recent venture is a boat line, Kelleys Island Ferry Boat Lines, Inc. which is currently the only ferry service between mainland Marblehead and Kelleys Island. Both Seaway Marina and the dock landing for the passenger ferry are located near the downtown commercial district, along a sidewalk-lined drive of one of the prettiest neighborhoods. The short block and a half walk from the ferry boat along the lake shore passes the Kelley Mansion, Inscription Rock, the three story frame Himmelein House, Crickett Inn (formerly the Himmelein/Sun home), and the downtown Memorial Park.

Mr. Palladino also owns property near the Seaway Marina that he operates as a farm, with chickens, cattle, and horses. The farm runs north all the way from East Lakeshore Drive by Seaway Marina to Woodford Road. He has an interest in organic food and his cattle are raised organically. The Palladinos also have additional property and homes around Kelleys Island. James Palladino has

1938 Buffalo fire engine used in parades by the Kelleys Island Volunteer Fire Department.

been an animal lover throughout his life. As a boy, he saw the circus when he visited his grandparents near Cleveland, Ohio, and as a member of the Kelleys Island Chamber of Commerce, he enjoys making it possible for others to recall childhood memories by sponsoring the Kelly Miller traveling circus that has visited the Island every August during recent years.

In 2004, James Palladino's son August, purchased the historic Casino bar and restaurant located at the foot of Division Street on the lake. The building dates from 1876 when Jacob Rush built a boat house with an upper story for open air dancing. At this time Rush also owned the Island House Hotel across the street. After the Island House burned August Schaedler bought the property, along with the boat house. Further down the hill was the thriving steam boat dock and store. In 1901 Charles Himmelein purchased the building and remodeled it to become the Casino. The Casino, then and now included private dockage and a landing for excursion and ferry boats. During the summer the *Jet Express* and the *Goodtime*, both tourist boats, dock for loading and discharging passengers. The available services include golf cart rental and a bar-restaurant. August Palladino has continued to make renovations both on the building and in the dock area.

Edward Kuchar also sees opportunity on Kelleys Island, but of a different nature than most. He purchases older homes and restores them, re-creating the look of the Island before 1950. Through his preservation efforts many homes have been saved from decay or "modern renovation." They act as historic markers in Island neighborhoods that continue the flavor and the look of the Island community at

Boats docked in Portside Marina on the south shore.

its apex, when it was vital and energetic, and populated by hard-working and flourishing families. Edward Kuchar preserves the past as he remembers it from his youth during summers on the Island with his family.

Besides owning a number of residences, and the Kelley Mansion, he also has preserved the Becker Barn and pasture, one of the last working farms on the Island, and farm property with homes and out buildings on the west side from the Dodge and Kastning families. Every building that he purchases is renewed by his attention.

A recent change to the downtown is the expansion of the Portside Marina. Spurred on by the continuous need for dockage, this downtown marina has been expanded greatly since 2000. The Charles Martin Sr. native limestone contemporary house facing the lake was renovated to transform it from residential to commercial property and attach it to the marina complex. Portside Marina now hosts dockage for private boats in a combination of slips and tie offs. Marina patrons have the usual amenities along with a small gift shop dockside. The marina's location on the south shore near the foot of Division Street makes it near to the downtown area, close to a variety of restaurants, bars, food stores, the Chamber of Commerce and shopping.

The Kelleys Island House Restaurant, formerly the "Island House," is in a historic building, once the home of Henry Trieschman. The 1876 house is a mixture of Italianate and folk Victorian. Since it became a commercial enterprise around the 1960's, it has had a number of owners. The current proprietors are Terry Kranyak and his wife Beth. They also own a modern bed and breakfast on McGettigan Road. Terry serves the community as a member of the Board of Trustees of Public Affairs.

Kelleys Island hosts a number of events through the summer months, every week, April through October. The Chamber of Commerce has organized a number of annual events. Islandfest occurs in July and features an old-fashioned street dance and fireworks. Other Chamber activities include a Welcome Back Fish Fry in April, 5-K and 10-K Runs in June, a traveling circus in August, and Treasure Island Day in September which consists of Island-wide yard sales. September is traditionally a pleasant, warm month on the Island. The Kelleys Island Landowners Association (KILA) sponsors Homecoming at the Village Pavilion in August. It is a time to return to Kelleys Island to meet with old friends and make new ones. The Kelleys Island Historical Association (KIHA) sponsors the Butterfly Festival in September, to commemorate the Monarch Butterfly that has used Kelleys Island for years as a migratory stop on its way to Mexico.

On the south shore on a typical summer day, the lake is alive with activity between Kelleys Island and the mainland. Usually two ferries are passing one another; there may be a large ore carrier in transit or docked at Marblehead taking on stone, and riders on personal watercraft are trailing huge plumes of water as they traverse the distance from the mainland or just play off shore. Large tourist boats like the *Goodtime* or *Jet Express* dock at the Casino to discharge passengers, and numerous fishing boats, sailboats, and motor boats move in every direction as they head out for the day or head in to dock. In the early morning and late afternoon, you may see the *Pelee Islander*, a Canadian passenger boat, on her way from Canada to the port of Sandusky. There is an air of expectation everywhere as new arrivals and seasoned visitors explore and re-discover the magic of the Island in an inland sea.

Seagulls resting along the north shore.

Most of the Kelleys Island shoreline is rock. Sometimes the rocks are small and well worn "skipping stones" and in other areas they may be rough, large, or completely flat shelves.

Large rocks along the north shore form windows to the lake and beyond.

Bibliography

A special thank you is owed to my mother, Cecilia Ann (Riedy) Brown, who patiently answered all my questions about what life had been like on Kelleys Island.

Personal interviews with Dottie Simonds about the Villa; Kurt Boker about himself, his brother Dr. Heinz Boker, and geology and natural history; Joe Corso about his art; Laura Jean and Frank Pohorence about the Orthodox Church and Ice Boating; Charles Martin, Jr.; Florence McKillips; Russell Matso; Benjamin Elfers on fishing; Jeff Grashel, Plant Manager for Lafarge Kelleys Island Quarry; Frances Minshall and Werner Minshall on Minshall family history; Robert Erne and Geraldine Betzenheimer; Joanne Young, director of the Kelleys Island 4-H camp; Tim Richardson, director of Camp Patmos; Carmen Palladino on the quarry and the Kelleys Island Ferry Boat Line; Robert Overcasher on the airport and Charles L. Herndon on his art. A very special thank you goes to Sandy Alexander for her collaboration and guidance.

Bailey, Thomas A. The American Pageant, Second Edition. Boston: D.C. Heath and Company, 1961.

Boker, Kurt. "A History of Kelley's Island: The Kurt E. Boker Collection, Binder: Commercial Fishing/Transportation."

Boker, Kurt. "A Unique 3000-Year History of the Kelley's Pond Area."

Bowe, Lulu M. and Herdendorf, Charles E. "ODNR pamphlet on the Glacial Grooves." Put-In-Bay, Ohio: The Ohio State University, Franz Theodore Stone Laboratory, Ohio Sea Grant Program.

Brown, Lillian. "Retired Art Professor Returns Each Summer To Kelleys Island." Toledo Blade, November 18, 1947.

Elfers, A.F. Scenic, Historic, Classic Kelley's Island. Kelleys's Island, Ohio: A.F. Elfers, 1913.

Herndon, Charles. July 15, 2006. <http://www.charlesherndon.com>

Hills, Norman. A History of Kelleys Island, Ohio. Norman E. Hills, 1925.

Huntington, George C. "Historical Sketch of Kelleys Island." Given at a Regular Meeting of the Fire Lands Historical Society on March 11, 1862. The Firelands Pioneer, Volume IV, June 1863, pp 30-49.

Kelleys Island, A Tour Guide. Kelleys Island Historical Association. 1992.

Kelleys Island Memorial Day Program from 1924.

Krebs, Christine D. "An Example of a Subsurface Random Sampling Strategy: the Kelleys Island Survey Project." Thesis submission to the Division of Graduate Education and Research of the University of Cincinnati, 1976.

Kuchar, Edward. "Kelleys Life", November-December, 2001; June, 2001; July, 2001, August 2000, Nov/Dec 2004.

"Lafarge Kelleys Island Community Newsletter." April 2005.

"Lafarge Kelleys Island Open House." Fall 2005.

Linhardt, Becky. Kelleys Island An Island for all Seasons. Kelleys Cove, Inc., 1995.

Luebke, Grace. Elmore, Ohio - A History Preserved, Grace Luebke, 1975, re-printed by the Elmore Historical Society, 1997.

Martin, Jessie A. The Beginnings and Tales of the Lake Erie Islands. Jessie A. Martin, 1990.

Martin, Jessie A. A History and Some Tales of Kelleys Island, Ohio. Minneapolis: T.S. Denison & Company, Inc., 1975.

Morrison, Paul Cross. "Kelleys Island, Ohio: An Economy in Transition". Economic Geography, Vol. 1.26, No. 2, April 1950.

"Mr. Shay's Powerful Little Locomotive." Heartland Hills. 4 Oct. 1006. <http://www.geocities.com/Heartland/Hills/1444/ephraim.htm?20064>

Norona, Delf. "The Kelleys Island Printed Townmark." R.A. 532, period of article 1851-60, The Chronicle, Vol 24, No. 4, November 1972.

ODNR. Kelleys Island State Park - North Pond Nature Preserve, pamphlet published by ODNR in cooperation with the Kelleys Island Audubon Society.

Official West Virginia State Parks and Forests web site. 7 Oct. 2006. <http://www.wvstateparks.com/shay100.htm>

Pape, Kevin and Johannsen, Kyle, complied by. Ohio Historic Inventory, ERI-1619. 1985.

Pecke, Hewson L. A Standard History of Erie County, Ohio. Chicago and New York: Lewis Publishing Company. Vol. I, 1916, p. 334.

Rainey, Lee. "The Shays of Kelleys Island." Railroad Model Craftsman. December 1986, pp. 73-77.

Ross, Harry H. Enchanting Isles of Erie. Harry H. Ross, 1949.

Secretary of State of Ohio. Journal of Incorporations from the Secretary of State.

Village of Kelleys Island Ordinance 1998-O-41

Wendt, Gordon. In the Wake of the "Walk-in-the-Water, Second Edition. Commercial Printing Company, June 22, 1984, Second Ed., January 1995.

"Western Lake Erie Nautical Chart." ODNR, Division of Wildlife. 1991.

Photo Credits:

The photographs, drawings, and artwork reproduced in this book are under copyright by the photographers and artists and may not be reproduced in any form without permission in writing from the photographers and artists.

Arnold Scheele, page 69, still life oil painting is in the collection of Diane Nickles; marine oil painting is in the collection of the William Johnson family.

Becky Linhardt, photo (Himmelein House) on page 52

Charles Herndon, page 65, sculptures are in the collection of the artist

Cheri Harte, photos on pages 69 and 70

Claudia Brown: original photos–page opposite Table of Contents, pages II, 2, 3 (2 photos), 4 (2 photos), 5 (2 photos), 6 (Inscription Rock), 13, 14, 16, 23, 25 (4 photos), 26, 27, 28 (2 photos), 29 (trail), 30 (2 photos), 32 (Kelley Hall), 33, 34, 36 (State Park), 37 (3 photos), 38, 40 (St. Michael Church–2 photos), 43, 48, 49, 51,

On the east shore, the rocks are flat tables of limestone that extend into the lake.

53, 54 (Koster Dock), 56 (ice shanties), 57, 58 (maple trees & icy lake), 59 (4 photos), 60 (4 photos), 61, 62, 68, 71 (2 photos), 72, 75, front and back covers; Drawings– pages 4 (fossils), 7 (map 2007), 15 (Irad and Datus Kelley); photos of artwork–pages 66 and 67, originals are in the collection of the artist; photos from the collection of Claudia Brown–dedication page photo, pages 1, 15 (Division St. postcard), 40 (Congregational Church), 45 (3 photos), 47 (2 postcards), 54 (trap net fishermen), 55, 56 (sturgeon), photo of Walter Brown in afterward

DeBoard Collection, photo of the Kelley Mansion on page 50

Eric Bruce (photo of winery ruins), page 22

Henry Dischinger, page 63, oil paintings are in the collection of Diane Nickles

Joe Corso, of paintings, page 29 (woods–collection of the artist), page 31 (downtown–collection of J. and G. Finger) and page 64 in the collection of the artist

Leon Heinl, watercolors on pages 22 (Kelleys Island Winery–collection of Nancy St. Julian), and 40 (Zion Church–collection of JoAnn Dusseau)

R. B. Hayes Presidential Center/Charles E. Frohman Collection: photos on pages 6 (drawing of Inscription Roack), 7 (Cunningham's map), 8, 10, 11, 17, 18, 19, 32 (the Lodge), 36 (Lime Kilns), 39, and 44

Sandy Alexander, photos on pages 58 (Dottie Simonds and ice), 21 (Monarch Winery); both in her private collection

William D. Gorchester, antique engraving, page 20

A special thank you to readers of the book drafts: Sandy Alexander, Dottie Simonds, Cecilia Ann Brown, Diane Hughes Nickles, Geraldine Erne Betzenheimer and Kurt Boker.

A very special thank you to Arti Mader for her professional editing of the manuscript.

Afterword

A special thank you goes to Sandy and Don Alexander, who asked me to write this update to their previous book on Kelleys Island. They were benevolent taskmasters, allowing me to weave family and personal information into their vision of the book. We have tried to include some people that have not been included in previous books about Kelleys Island. We realized early in the task that it was impossible to include everyone and so we have included people that have been important to the Island or have touched our lives in some way. For my part, where appropriate, I have tried to include at least a mention of some of the family names that were important at one time to the Island, but no longer exist here. As a blood descendant of many Island families, I have realized how quickly names disappear and memories are forgotten. In a way, this book is a small effort towards the memory of those who gave their blood and sweat over a lifetime to the development of Kelleys Island. As one last indulgence I am including here the names of my forebears: Brown, Dischinger, Riedy, Feddersen, Klevens, Kastning, Dodge, Myers, Bookerman, and those they and their descendants married: Huntington, Kelley, Hauser, Lincoln, McKillips, Schardt, Hughes, Dwelle, Titus, Catanaugh, Emlinger, Ward, Lange, Erne, Hamilton, Matso, Betzenheimer, Bickley, Blatt, Duignan, Gerlach, and of my God parents, Helen (Verock) and Joseph Mervo—all good Kelleys Island names.

Walter Brown in a United Fish Co. boat. The boats were built in Sandusky for use in the pound fishing industry.